FIRST EASTER

FIRST EASTER

The True and Unfamiliar Story
in Words and Pictures

Paul L. Maier

1817

HARPER & ROW, PUBLISHERS
New York, Hagerstown, San Francisco, London

For my mother

HULDA A. MAIER

who first told me

about the first Easter

Biblical quotations in this book, where identified, are from the Revised Standard Version, which is copyright 1946 and 1952 by the Division of Christian Education of the National Council of the Churches of Christ in the United States of America. The other quotations are paraphrased by the author.

Photographs are by the author, except for those credited, which are published by permission of the agencies cited.

STANDARD BOOK NUMBER: 06-065397-3

LIBRARY OF CONGRESS CATALOG CARD NUMBER: 72-81346

Designed by Lydia Link

77 78 79 80 81 10 9 8 7 6 5 4

CONTENTS

ILLUSTRATIONS

COLOR PLATES

PREFACE

Since Jesus' final week in Jerusalem is probably the most familiar story in the history of Western civilization, to retell it for the purpose of adding new information and insights would seem rank presumption. And yet these pages reflect historical and archaeological research that has taken old but overlooked evidence as well as new discoveries to try to illumine the moving story of the first Holy Week and flesh out some of its important details.

I am grateful that the same approach has met with such a generous critical and popular reception in the case of my *First Christmas*. This companion volume is a Lent-Easter documentary that also aims to provide some information that is well known, some little known, and some new for the days marking the culmination, rather than the beginning, of Jesus' career. No liberties were taken with the facts, which are documented in the Notes at the end of the book, most of which involve original sources.

I am especially indebted to Western Michigan University for the Faculty Research Grant that assisted this investigation, as well as to Lois Sohn Glock of the Albright Institute in Jerusalem (American School for Oriental Research) and Dr. George H. Liebenow of Xavier University for their kindnesses.

P.L.M.

Western Michigan University

1

UP TO JERUSALEM

A great crowd who had come to the feast heard that Jesus was coming to Jerusalem. So they took branches of palm trees and went out to meet him, crying, "Hosanna! Blessed is he who comes in the name of the Lord, even the King of Israel!"

JOHN 12:12–13

IT WAS, QUITE LITERALLY, "the week that changed the world." A later age would call it Holy Week and bestow names like Palm Sunday, Good Friday, and Easter on its days. But, soon after it happened, the crucial character of Jesus' final visit to Jerusalem was realized. Three of the Gospels devote a full third of their content to reporting this week, while the Fourth dedicates its entire last half.

And rippling across the rest of these records is a sense of inevitability about this life: Jesus of Nazareth was a man born to die—not merely in the normal sense, but with some special significance—an overtone, a leitmotiv that begins in the Christmas story and recurs throughout the three and one-half years of Jesus' public ministry.

Sometimes it was only a veiled hint. On other occasions, Jesus spelled it out directly, like the time he gathered his disciples together and announced their Passover plans: "Behold, we are going up to Jerusalem, and everything that is written of the Son of man by the prophets will be accomplished. For he will be delivered to the Gentiles, and will be mocked and shamefully treated and spit upon; they will scourge him and kill him, and on the third day he will rise" (Lk. 18:31–33).

As at other times, the disciples greeted this statement with a collective sag of the jaw. They simply could not grasp the Teacher's intent, and the positive note on which Jesus' statement ended was merely obscured by the almost suicidal nature of the rest of it.

The Unteachable Twelve

The even dozen who followed Jesus from his earliest public ministry in Galilee seemed to have one thing in common despite their varied backgrounds: a reliable dullness that hardly ever failed to misinterpret Jesus' message, and that usually asked him the naïve question at the wrong time. Occasionally the disciples even interfered with his mission, blocking children from access to him, or trying to dissuade him from his course. If Socrates chose a Plato as disciple, and Plato an Aristotle, might Jesus of Nazareth not have been a shade more selective in his choice of followers?

Perhaps it was just as well that he chose as he did. The Twelve represent all of inquiring humanity, not just the sages, and their reactions—however plodding or puzzled—are our own. Particularly their very human emotions of fear or wonder, sorrow or elation at various times in Jesus' ministry add a convincing touch to the New Testament records. Were the disciples, then, really dolts? Not unless mankind itself is doltish. And after the overpowering experience of the first Easter, something transformed these men into brilliant and courageous apostles of the new faith, a change so dramatic that it must be dealt with later in these pages.

Biographies of the Twelve are hardly possible. There were two pairs of brothers who were fishermen: Peter and Andrew, James and John. A government official named Matthew was a tax collector, while, quite oppositely, another disciple named Simon had

probably been active *against* the government in the Zealot movement, though there is no indication that he continued these activities as a disciple. All were Galileans except for Judas Iscariot,
the later traitor, who was probably from Judea. The empirical
Thomas, who had a skeptic's mind—or was it a scientist's?—had
a twin brother who has vanished from history. But the other
disciples are as transparent as the breezes of Palestine: Philip,
Bartholomew, James Ben-Alphaeus, and Thaddaeus.

Whatever they may have thought of Jesus' announced Passover
plans, there was no thought of opposing them once the Teacher
had "set his face to go to Jerusalem," as Luke puts it (9:51).
Probably Jesus was only speaking in riddles again or in metaphor,
they reasoned, an old habit of his. They had all been to Jerusalem
before and returned safely to Galilee. So it would be again.

A Base at Bethany

Their eighty-mile journey south took them via the Jordan valley to sunny Jericho, the last halting station for pilgrims from the
north country who traveled to Jerusalem for the great Jewish
festivals. Here Jesus had his famous appointments with dwarfish,
tree-climbing Zacchaeus, the overeager tax collector, and a blind
beggar named Bartimaeus. The New Testament reports both of
them cured—in their separate fashions. And so the week that
altered history had a rather ordinary prelude, typical of other
days in Jesus' career.

Since Jericho lay 825 feet *below* sea level near the Dead Sea,
while Jerusalem was perched on the hilly backbone of Palestine
some 2,500 feet above sea level, Jesus' statement about going *"up
to Jerusalem"* was quite literally true. The final leg of their journey was a dusty trek that twisted its way upward through barren
hills and ravines in the Judean badlands surrounding the Holy
City. Usually the roadway was desolate enough to attract highway
robbers, and it was no accident that Jesus had chosen exactly this
setting for his parable about the Good Samaritan. But now it was

becoming choked with crowds of Passover pilgrims who were singing the traditional "songs of ascent" as they trudged upward toward Jerusalem behind their snorting and smelly beasts of burden.

Jesus and the disciples were aiming for one of the eastern suburbs of Jerusalem, a town called Bethany, which would serve as their lodging place and base of operations for the coming week. There were several important reasons for staying here rather than in the capital. For one thing, finding accommodations in the Holy City would have been next to impossible. Jerusalem, which normally had a population of some 50,000, was at least tripling in size because of the vast influx of pilgrims celebrating the Passover, and the city was ringed with tents. Then, too, Jesus, who was popular with the crowds, was quite vulnerable apart from them, and his adversaries might have come by night to arrest him earlier than they did had they been able to locate his place of residence inside Jerusalem.

The Teacher also had friends living in Bethany, very intimate friends. The sisters Mary and Martha, along with their brother Lazarus, had played host to Jesus and his entourage several times earlier, and this is the one spot in Palestine where he could truly relax. A short time earlier, Jesus had even worked the ultimate sign on Lazarus, according to the Fourth Gospel, raising him from the dead after four days' entombment.

Since Bethany lay just on the other side of the Mount of Olives from Jerusalem, the still-fresh news of this event had a direct and double effect on the events of Holy Week. Those who believed that Jesus had truly raised Lazarus planned a delirious welcome for him in Jerusalem. But those who thought Jesus a magician or imposter quickly set their plans to capture him into high gear, lest the pseudo-Messiah attract too large a following and compel Roman intervention.

While news of Jesus' approach was going from mouth to mouth in Jerusalem, he himself spent one of his last happy nights in

Bethany at a dinner party given by his friends. The scene of Mary anointing the feet of Jesus after supper and wiping them with her hair is familiar enough, particularly because of Judas Iscariot's grumbling reaction: "Why was this ointment not sold for three hundred denarii and given to the poor?"

"Poor Judas" may have been more appropriate, since, as treasurer of the Twelve, he regularly pilfered from the group purse and was not at all concerned about the poor. In reprimanding Judas for his misplaced charity, Jesus closed with an amazing statement: "Truly, I say to you, wherever the gospel is preached in the whole world, what she has done will be told in memory of her" (Mk. 14:9). To suggest that news of the event would ever extend this far would seem presumptuous predicting, whether Jesus himself said it or, as critics might claim, Mark put the words in his mouth. But about a century ago, with the full missionary expansion of Christianity, this prophecy was quite literally fulfilled.

A Royal Reception

Early Sunday morning, Jesus made his baldly public entry into Jerusalem. It was the end of all privacy and safety, and the beginning of what would be an inevitable collision course with the priestly and political authorities in the land. His irrevocable step was taken deliberately, with every consideration for the consequences, for otherwise he might simply have slipped unceremoniously into the city along with the thousands of pilgrims.

The word was out. Crowds had started gathering even in Bethany for a glimpse of the rabbi from Galilee as well as the Lazarus whom he had revived. In the neighboring hamlet of Bethphage, a she-ass was waiting to transport Jesus, according to his own specifications. And then the triumphal procession began, accompanied by shouting and singing from the throngs of people lining the roadsides. They threw down their garments on the pathway

Palm Sunday procession entering the Via Dolorosa in Jerusalem.

to cushion his ride—an Oriental custom still observed on occasion—as well as palm fronds, the symbol of triumph, paving his way with nature's green.

"Hosanna to the Son of David! Blessed is he who comes in the name of the Lord! Hosanna in the Highest!" The exultant shouts accompanied Jesus along the entire route down the Mount of Olives, which is still used each Palm Sunday by a procession of Christians carrying palm branches. Just skirting the Garden of Gethsemane, Jesus and his entourage finally crossed the Brook Kidron and entered Jerusalem, probably via the Golden Gate, the northeastern portal of the Temple enclave, which has since been walled up.

What did it all mean? Had Jesus perhaps arranged for the donkey because he was tired? Hardly. It was morning, and on other occasions he was a tireless walker. It was a gesture of humility, many have suggested, for the ass was the common beast of burden of the time in contrast to the superior horse or gilded chariot used in Roman triumphs.

If so, the gesture quickly conferred a quite opposite flavor to the occasion. The prophet Zechariah had foretold the arrival of the Messianic king in Jerusalem via this humble conveyance (9:9), and here the crowd was according a wildly triumphant reception to one whom they hailed as "the son of David," a loaded name used at a loaded place, for many Jews expected the Messiah figure to be declared as king on that very Mount of Olives.

The priestly establishment in Jerusalem witnessed the procession also, catching and perhaps enlarging on any political overtones in the demonstration. Might not the waving of palm branches be symbolic, since the palm was the national emblem of an independent Palestine? These were Jewish flags! What if Jesus should actually claim to be heir of King David in a restored Judean monarchy? After all, the multitude was lavishing such dizzying phrases on him as "the King of Israel."

Caiaphas, the high priest, must have cast a worried glance westward in the direction of Herod's palace, where the Roman governor, Pontius Pilate, had just arrived to be on hand for the Passover in case any demonstrations—*such as this one*—might get out of hand. He must also have marveled at the brazen effrontery of the rabbi from Galilee: the very man for whom arrest notices had been posted across the land was coming directly into Jerusalem in the most obvious manner possible.

2

INTRIGUE AND CONSPIRACY

"It is expedient for you that one man should die for the people, and that the whole nation should not perish." . . . So from that day on they took counsel how to put him to death.

JOHN 11:50–53

ACCORDING TO THE USUAL STORY of Holy Week, the high priests, Pharisees, Sadducees, Herodians, scribes, and other opponents of Jesus suddenly decided to seize the opportunity of arresting him once he had been foolhardy enough to show up in Jerusalem, and they began plotting in earnest. This is incorrect. The conspiracy against Jesus had been building for at least three years, and the sources record seven instances of official plotting against him, two efforts at arrest, and three assassination attempts before the events of Holy week.

A formal decision to arrest Jesus had in fact been made several months earlier, probably at a secret session of the Sanhedrin, the great Judean senate. Jerusalem had been rocking with news that Jesus had supposedly raised Lazarus of Bethany from the dead, and people were feverish with excitement over the fact that Jesus was performing exactly the great signs expected of the Messiah, the religio-political figure who, in the popular interpretation, was to deliver the land from foreign domination.

"So if Jesus is allowed to continue performing his signs, however he does them," opined one Sanhedrist, "he will win over our entire population, and then the Romans will come and destroy our Temple and our nation."

It was the high priest, Joseph Caiaphas, who quickly raised his hands to silence the growing hubbub that followed this comment, and now he skewered the mood of alarm with pontifical authority: "You do not understand, my brothers, that it is expedient for you that one man should die for the people, and that the whole nation should not perish." For the public safety, the sacrifice of a single troublemaker was not too high a price to pay.

The Fourth Gospel concludes this crucial scene with a revealing statement: "Now the chief priests and the Pharisees had given orders that if any one knew where he [Jesus] was, he should let them know, so that they might arrest him" (11:57).

We may, in fact, have some idea of how the arrest notice read. A rabbinical tradition recorded in the Talmud spells out the indictment against Yeshu Hannosri (Hebrew for "Jesus the Nazarene"). Combined with the New Testament, the notice can be reconstructed as follows:

WANTED: YESHU HANNOSRI

He shall be stoned because he has practiced sorcery and enticed Israel to apostasy. Anyone who can say anything in his favor, let him come forward and plead on his behalf. Anyone who knows where he is, let him declare it to the Great Sanhedrin in Jerusalem.

According to legal custom at the time, a court crier had to announce publicly or post such an official handbill in the larger towns of Judea about forty days prior to a trial. Small wonder that there was some debate over whether Jesus would dare to appear in Jerusalem for the next Passover. But the discussion ended abruptly on Palm Sunday.

As the Passion story has been retold through the centuries, the picture has become more and more "contrasty" in the telling. Jesus and the disciples are the gleaming protagonists marching resignedly into the jaws of mortal danger, while their opponents are painted in progressively ugly hues: Pilate is a muddy russet (due to admixture of coward's yellow), Caiaphas is murky sepia, and Judas is Devil's black. But where are the grays and medium tones that certainly existed among the enemies of Jesus?

They opposed him for various reasons, and some—it must be admitted—were acting in good faith. The high priest Caiaphas was a worldly wise Sadducee whose overriding policy was to maintain the uneasy compromise between Jewish and Roman authority in Palestine. Now in his fifteenth year as high priest, Caiaphas, like any Jew, would have preferred an independent Judea controlled by God and his vicegerents, the priestly establishment, but he had the political sense to realize that Rome's was not a passing power in the eastern Mediterranean, and the road to success lay in continuing cooperation with the Empire and its representative, Pontius Pilate.

Because there had been a dozen uprisings in Palestine since Pompey first conquered the land in 63 B.C.—most of them subdued by Roman force—another Messianic rebellion under Jesus of Nazareth would only shatter the precarious balance of authority and, bleeding Rome's patience dry, might lead to direct occupation by Roman legions. For *political* reasons, therefore, Jesus would have to be dealt with.

There were, of course, important *religious* reasons as well: people were hailing the Teacher from Galilee as something more than a man, and Jesus was not blunting this blasphemous adulation. The wonders he supposedly performed to mislead the multitudes were either hoaxes, they reasoned, or of demonic origin.

And for many of his opponents there were also corrosive *personal* reasons for hating the Nazarene: the Pharisees in particular had been bested by Jesus in public debate and then called such epithets as: "whitewashed tombs," "vipers," and "devourers of widows' houses." Rankling with humiliation, they only too happily conspired with the scribes, elders, and chief priests.

A reconstruction of the great Temple, in the model of ancient Jerusalem designed by Prof. M. Avi-Yonah at the Holyland Hotel in Jerusalem. To the upper left are the three northern towers of the Palace of Herod in the western part of the Holy City.

A Monday Housecleaning

And finally, now, there were even *economic* motives for opposing Jesus. The great, gleaming Temple in Jerusalem, King Herod's one great favor to the city, was Jesus' most tangible connection with the Old Testament and his own past. Here he had been presented as a baby and redeemed by Joseph and Mary. Here, too, he had displayed dazzling brilliance as a twelve-year-old prodigy, and just now the Temple enclave was in final stages of completion.

One of the thrilling moments for today's visitor to Palestine is to notice that, despite the terrible, repeated destructions of Jerusalem over the centuries since that time, great blocks of Herodian masonry—original stones from Jesus' day—are *still* supporting the vast Temple platform at the southeast and southwest corners, on which the Muslim Dome of the Rock now stands. The blocks are instantly recognizable because they are not only enormous, but handsomely dressed with flat, raised faces and sunken margins about six inches wide. The disciples thought even Jesus should have been impressed. Said one of them, "Look, Teacher, what wonderful stones and what wonderful buildings!" (Mk. 13:1).

But what impressed Jesus was the commercialization taking place inside the Temple. Some of it was inevitable. The half-shekel contributions to the Temple would require conversion from foreign currency or change from domestic, so there were various banking and moneychanging tables in the outer courts of the Temple to accommodate worshipers. And who would prefer dragging a lamb down from Galilee for the Passover sacrifice when one could be purchased more conveniently from livestock dealers at the Temple? There were also pigeon stalls for those who could afford only the minimum sacrifice, and a hodgepodge of tourist shops and sidewalk merchants also infested the premises, as in today's Jerusalem.

Yet this profiting on holy ground infuriated Jesus. The boisterous haggling, the clinking of coins, the groaning and bleating from oxen and sheep, to say nothing of the endless clucking of the doves, was, if anything, distracting from the solemnity of worship, quite apart from the inevitable stench. Jesus made a whip out of cords and lashed away at the dealers and their livestock, probably causing an animal stampede out of the Temple courts. Then he overturned the tables of the moneychangers with the famous cry, "It is written, 'My house shall be called a house of prayer'; but you make it a den of robbers" (Mt. 21:13).

Easily one of the most graphic pictures of Holy Week, Jesus' cleansing of the Temple is also one of the more controversial. Scholars have divided themselves into three camps on this episode. Some insist the entire scene is mythical and could never have happened, since the many Temple police in the precincts would quickly have dealt with so obvious a troublemaker. Yet, by the time the guards arrived in any force, the whole affair was a *fait accompli,* and they would not have dared apprehend Jesus at the time because of his popularity with the thousands of Passover pilgrims, who were likely cheering him on from the sidelines.

Other writers find in this violence the act of a Zealot and would make Jesus a member of that revolutionary political resistance movement. But flailing away at merchants, moneychangers, and animals rather than at Roman auxiliaries was a rather pathetic way to start a rebellion. And so the balance of scholars conclude that this was an isolated act of Jesus that happened more or less as described in the New Testament, which certainly seems the most logical conclusion.

The Verbal Snares

News of this scene cut the priestly establishment to the quick. What might well be called "Annas, Caiaphas, and Co." controlled all concessions on the Temple premises, and, while one day's loss was not that significant, Jesus was setting a precedent

The southeastern corner of the Temple platform in Jerusalem, showing great blocks of Herodian masonry nearly to the top. The walls continue underground in a vast substructure 24 meters below the present surface.

that might well rouse the rabble to future assaults on the Temple and disrupt worship and sacrifice. He would have to be dealt with —immediately.

But how? Arresting him by daylight was not feasible because of his obvious popularity with the people. Insulated by them, Jesus was even showing up at the Temple on a daily basis, teaching crowds that seemed to be able to listen to him for hours at a time. But precisely here he might be vulnerable, the Pharisees surmised. If he could be tripped up in his words or defeated in argument before the multitude—proved to be a false prophet— then his popular support would vanish.

This was the reasoning behind the astonishing confrontations in the Temple between Jesus and emissaries from the Pharisees and the sacerdotal aristocracy on Monday, Tuesday, and Wednesday of Holy Week. They might almost be styled "Jesus' final press conferences," for he had to field a withering fusillade of questions from bright minds that, however, were aiming not for news so much as to discredit what they thought a pseudo-prophet.

Yet Jesus parried each challenge with devastating success. Questions about his own authority to teach and teasers on multiple remarriage and the greatest commandment of the law were answered to the embarrassment of the interrogators. The most loaded query of all, certainly, was this: "Tell us, Teacher, is it lawful to pay taxes to Caesar, or not?"

It was a cruel alternative. A Yes would have prevented any trouble with the political authorities but reduced Jesus in the popular mind to a Rome-serving lackey. A No would have pleased the crowd, but reports of Jesus' treason would have been conveyed immediately to Pontius Pilate.

Like the best of teachers, Jesus was not above using visual aids. Calling for a coin, he asked whose image and inscription it bore. At the expected answer he merely replied, "Then render to Caesar the things that are Caesar's, and to God the things that are God's" (Mt. 22:21).

Prizes for everyone! Rome could hardly find the remark sedi-
tious, while the Jews knew the statement meant not 50 per cent
to God but more like 99 per cent, since the human being be-
longed to God as his creation.

The attempts to humiliate Jesus before the multitudes had
failed. His opponents would now have to use other means.

3

A LAST SUPPER

Judas, who betrayed him, said, "Is it I, Master?" He said to him, "You have said so."

Now as they were eating, Jesus took bread, and blessed, and broke it, and gave it to the disciples and said, "Take, eat; this is my body." And he took a cup, and when he had given thanks he gave it to them, saying, "Drink of it, all of you; for this is my blood. . . ."

MATTHEW 26:25–28

JUDAS ISCARIOT OCCUPIES a wholly unique place in history: deservedly or not, he ranks as the greatest popular villain of all time. In his *Divine Comedy,* Dante places him in the deepest chasm of the inferno, where Satan munches on him as a steady diet. If this seems too medieval, modern opinion on Judas is not much more sophisticated in some parts of the world. Each Good Friday in Mexico, the people ignite firecrackers that sizzle and pop until the burning fuse reaches a hideous, powder-stuffed Judas doll that finally blows up. And Greeks on the island of Corfu, in a swelling chorus of curses, pitch great quantities of crockery down a steep hill in an imaginary stoning of Judas.

He was the son of Simon Iscariot, about whom nothing is known. Scholars have puzzled over the meaning of Iscariot, and one of the most frequent definitions is *ish-Kerioth,* Hebrew for "man from Kerioth." But the location of this village is uncertain, and another explanation is gaining some currency: Iscariot may be a corruption of the Latin *sicarius,* which means "assassin" or "murderer." The Sicarii were a radical, terrorist sect among the anti-Roman Jews who felled their enemies by mingling with them

29

in crowds, thrusting a quick dagger into their ribs, and then vanishing.

Whatever his background, Judas was one of the leaders of the Twelve, even though his name is cited last in the list of the disciples, for the Gospels were written only after his betrayal had degraded his memory. In fact, Judas was treasurer of the group, and was probably reclining next to Jesus in a place of honor at the Last Supper. But by this time he had already approached the chief priests with his infamous offer to betray Jesus.

The Need for an Insider

What were Judas' motives? Was it because Jesus had discovered his pilfering from the treasury and planned to expose him? Was he disappointed in Jesus' failure to declare himself a political Messiah who would free Palestine from Roman control? Was he disillusioned enough to deem him a false prophet? Or, in a masterpiece of strategy, was he trying to force Jesus into a vulnerable position where he would have to display his Messianic powers in order to deliver himself? The Teacher had eluded arrest before, and now he could do so in a great public show of supernatural force in the Holy City that would convince the nation once and for all.

Perhaps it was a combination of all these motives, or it could have been something so simple as avarice. After all, Judas did want to be paid for his information, and thirty pieces of silver was the agreed price, enough to buy a suit of clothes. Judas would profit, however pettily, and Jesus could always save himself if he chose.

But what intelligence could Judas possibly deliver to the priestly authorities? Some critics doubt that the betrayal story is historical, because Jesus was not in hiding: on the contrary, he was delivering daily lectures in the Temple. Since apprehending him before the crowds would have caused an uproar, however, the arrest would have to take place by night.

An ancient flight of stairs leading from the Upper City of Jerusalem down to the Kidron Valley. Jesus and the disciples may have used these steps on the way to Gethsemane.

Yet where in the tent city surrounding Jerusalem was Jesus staying? And how could he be seized at night without arousing his fellow Galileans encamped round about? And how could they be sure to arrest the right person when all men wore a beard, dressed approximately the same, and were blanketed by darkness? This was long before the day of wire-service photos and their universal identification of the famous. However, Judas' agreement to identify Jesus' nocturnal whereabouts, even to the point of singling him out with a kiss of greeting, nicely solved all these problems, and the pact was concluded.

Now it was Thursday, April 2, 33 A.D., a date that best corresponds to the various chronological clues in the sources. For the first time during Holy Week, it seems that Jesus stayed in Bethany rather than going into Jerusalem. How did he spend his final hours of freedom? Doubtless in the company of his intimate friends, including his mother Mary, who must have been on the scene since she stood at the foot of the cross the next day.

No later than noon, Jesus sent Peter and John into Jerusalem to make arrangements for their Passover meal. "A man carrying a jar of water will meet you," Jesus told them, and he would identify the house with an upper guest room where they would keep the feast. The recognition sign would be unusual enough, since in the East it was women who usually drew the water and carried it from wells in pitchers perched precariously on their heads, a common sight in Palestine to this day.

A Passover Seder?

At sundown, the Twelve gathered with Jesus for dinner in the upper room. But what they ate has been vigorously debated across the centuries since then, because the synoptic Gospels—Matthew, Mark, and Luke—state quite clearly that this was the Passover Seder or meal, whereas John insists that this was the day *before* the Passover. Numerous attempts have been made to harmonize these differences, some suggesting that the Passover may have been observed on two consecutive days that year, due to variant reckonings by the Pharisees and Sadducees, or the Judeans and Galileans. Others claim that Jesus celebrated an intentionally early Passover, knowing what would happen the next day.

Following the Johannine tradition, the Eastern Orthodox churches to this day celebrate Holy Communion with regular leavened bread, whereas the Roman Catholic sacrament uses *un*leavened bread wafers similar to what would have been eaten at a Passover meal. Lutherans and Anglicans generally follow the synoptic tradition also, while the rest of Protestantism uses either form.

But there can be no doubt that the mind of every Jew at this time was focused on the Passover festival, so the discrepancy may be nothing more serious than, for example, celebrating a Christmas dinner on either December 24 or 25. The Passover itself commemorated the liberation of the ancient Hebrews from their enslavement in Egypt. While the first-born male Egyptians were dying in the dreadful tenth plague, the Israelites were secure behind doorways marked with lamb's blood as they ate a dinner of unleavened bread, bitter herbs, and roast lamb, which had been cooked over an open fire on a spit made of pomegranate wood (Ex. 12).

The supper shared by Jesus and the disciples must have been similar—up to a point. Then a note of tension broke the happiness of the dinner as the Teacher enlarged on a point he had already made while giving the Twelve an object lesson in humility by washing their feet. He had said, "You are not all clean." Then, after another hint, he came out directly, "Truly, I say to you, one of you will betray me."

Innocently they all inquired, "Is it I, Lord?" Judas joined in the question lest he incriminate himself by silence.

Looking him coolly in the eye, Jesus replied, "You have said so.—What you are going to do, do quickly."

Hot with embarrassment, Judas rose from his reclining position at the table and skulked out of the room. Possibly Jesus had only whispered the identification, since the rest of the disciples merely thought Judas off on an errand.

Toward the close of the supper, Jesus introduced a momentous alteration into the usual Passover Seder. He took some of the remaining bread, blessed it and broke it, and then distributed it among his colleagues with the words, "Take, eat, this is my body." Wondering at his language, the disciples did just that.

Then he reached for the cup of red Passover wine standing in front of him. According to custom, it had been diluted, two parts of water to one of wine. Again he offered thanks and passed the chalice among them, saying, "Drink of it, all of you; for this is my blood of the new covenant, shed for many, for the remission of sins. Do this, as often as you drink it, in remembrance of me."

With these words, Jesus inaugurated what became the longest continuous meal in history, for soon his followers would begin celebrating what they later called The Lord's Supper or Holy Communion, in which someone, somewhere in the world, has been offering up bread and wine in a similar manner nearly every moment since.

The meaning of Jesus' words stems from a complex of ideas that lie at the very heart of Christianity. Just as in Old Testament worship the flesh and blood of a sacrificed victim were offered separately, so Jesus was to be the new paschal lamb offered in sacrifice for sin. This new covenant was intended to be a direct fulfillment of the old, which had been established after the Passover liberation from Egypt. God was offering man a fresh contract or agreement in Jesus: his sacrifice on the cross would bring liberation, not from Egypt, but from the slavery of sin. The supper also foreshadowed the Messianic banquet he would share with his followers in the future kingdom.

But all this was scarcely comprehended by the disciples at the time, and not until later would they reflect on Jesus' words and understand their meaning in full. For now, all they could do was wonder at the fresh tack taken by the Teacher and listen to his last discourses, which seemed strangely attuned to the future.

The Brook Kidron, looking south toward an olive grove in the
Gethsemane area and the lower reaches of the Mount of Olives.

Finally, they all sang a closing Passover hymn, and then Jesus uttered his magnificent concluding prayer, which began with ominous import: "Father, the hour has come. . . ." It had indeed. They filed out of the room and walked eastward through the darkened streets of Jerusalem toward the Mount of Olives.

4

IN THE GARDEN

And Jesus said to them, "Have you come out as against a robber, with
swords and clubs to capture me? Day after day I was with you in the
temple teaching, and you did not seize me. But let the scriptures be
fulfilled."

MARK 14:48–49

CERTAIN ANCIENT TRADITIONS place the upper room in the ele-
vated southwestern corner of Jerusalem, although the present
purported site for the Last Supper, an upper chamber of gothic
arches, is easily the least convincing holy place in Palestine. But
if Jesus and the disciples did dine somewhere in this quarter of
the city, they would doubtless have made their way over to
Gethsemane via a roadway winding around the southeastern corner of Jerusalem. A very ancient flight of steps descending toward
the Kidron valley has been excavated, which could very well have
been used by Jesus and the Eleven who filed after him.

There was some dialogue as the party made its way in and out
of the stark shadows cast by the full Passover moon, which had
now risen gloriously over the Mount of Olives to the east. With
what must have been a resigned sigh, Jesus said, "You will all fall
away because of me this night. . . . But after I am raised up, I will
go before you to Galilee."

Simon Peter, the big beloved fisherman who always managed
to get in the first word after Jesus said something, did not fail him
now. With a slightly demeaning gesture toward his colleagues, he
said, "Even if *they* all fall away because of you, I will never fall
away."

37

Shaking his head sadly, Jesus told him, "This very night, before the cock crows, you will deny me three times."

"Even if I must *die* with you, I'll not deny you," Peter objected. Not to be left out, and more than a little resentful at Peter's presumption, the other disciples quickly added their own promises of loyalty to the death.

Now they were crossing the Kidron, a brook that cuts through the valley separating the Temple platform from the Mount of Olives. Most of the time, this celebrated stream is nothing more than a dry ditch littered with boulders, but after a heavy rainfall the rivulet spumes with roiling waters that soon find their way into the Dead Sea. In Jesus' day, when the valley was several yards deeper, the brook would gurgle all spring.

They were walking toward a grove of olive trees nestled in the lower reaches of the Mount of Olives, a favorite haunt of Jesus and the Twelve. It was called Gethsemane, meaning "oil vat" or "oil press" in Aramaic, and somewhere in the garden the contrivance likely stood, its stone wheels reflecting a ghostly blue-white in the moonlight. Ancient olive presses are commonplace in Palestine to this day, for olive oil production was a major industry in Biblical times. A vertical stone wheel, driven by human or donkey power, rolled over the olives spread out on a flat, horizontal stone, which was grooved to let the oil trickle into a basin.

The Psychological Agony

When Jesus and his party entered the garden, the stage was set for the most human scene in the entire Passion story. Lenten preaching so often makes Jesus a larger-than-life figure who is completely in control of the tragic events swirling about him, as if playing out his role from a divine scenario whose glorious ending he knew well enough. Jesus the man is too often obscured by the Messianic Christ.

But Gethsemane shows the humanity of Jesus with astonishing

fidelity. He told his followers to stay in the grove while he went off a stone's throw to pray, for he had to be alone. Completely alone? Perhaps misery did love company, for he took the inner three disciples with him: Peter, James, and John. At any moment Judas and the arresting party were due in the garden, so he told them to warn him of their approach while he went a little farther off and prayed.

Falling on his face, he agonized, "My Father, if it be possible, let this cup pass from me; nevertheless, not as I will, but as thou wilt" (Mt. 26:39). For an omnipotent God, wasn't some alternate plan possible than the horror that lay immediately ahead? In fact, Jesus was wavering in his mission, because he was a man, too, and men waver when they stare into the jaws of death. If the story of Holy Week were a pious invention of writers who wanted to portray a superhero, this scene would never have been included. But, almost breathing with realism, it shows Jesus distractedly trying to interrupt his own agony by going over to check on the trio of disciples three different times. With unfailing consistency, they were sleeping each time.

Luke, the doctor, adds a medical detail in his account. During the psychological struggle of wills being waged in Jesus' mind, his perspiration "became like great drops of blood falling down upon the ground" (22:44). Because of the simile, too much should not be made of this statement, although, in cases of extreme stress, it is physiologically possible for the human body to sweat blood.

It was now between 10 and 11 P.M. Orion, the great winter constellation, was just setting in the northwest, its first-magnitude stars still visible through the bright moonlight. But the privacy of the Passion story ended at this moment. A clanking of men and arms was starting to shatter the hush of night. Quivering daggers of orange flame began stabbing the horizon to the west, and soon a procession of torches filed into the grove. Judas, at the head of an armed company of Temple guardsmen, walked over to Jesus and said, "Hail Master!" Then he gave him a kiss

The gnarled trunk of an ancient olive tree, perhaps 900 years old, standing in the traditional Garden of Gethsemane.

of greeting—whether on the hand or cheek is not known—the agreed signal identifying Jesus.

In his familiar reply, spoken contemptuously or sadly, Jesus asked, "Judas, would you betray the Son of man with a kiss?" Revulsion at the traitor's hypocritical gesture makes one almost instinctively wipe off his hand or cheek on reading the account.

The next moment, Simon Peter lunged for his sword to defend Jesus. Much derision has been heaped on the poor, impetuous fisherman for resorting to violence and then making such a mess of it, flailing away with one misguided thrust that merely slashed off the right ear of the high priest's servant Malchus. And yet the hopeless swipe is almost refreshing in a sense, the one token act of courage by any of the disciples in their otherwise dismal record of cowardice.

"No more of this!" Jesus quickly interposed, before everyone began swinging. "Put your sword into its sheath. Shall I not drink the cup which the Father has given me?" Again, only Luke adds the medical touch that Jesus then healed the wounded man. An early tradition claims, understandably, that this incident converted Malchus, who was likely of Idumaean extraction.

In his last free moment, Jesus could not resist taunting the crowd for clutching cudgels and swords as if hunting out a robber when just hours earlier they had not arrested him in the Temple. "But if you seek me, let these men go," he said, pointing to the disciples.

Huddling together in a shivering pool of fear at the edge of the grove, the Eleven took their cue and promptly fled from Gethsemane, abandoning their Teacher just one hour after their brave promises to the contrary. Then Jesus was seized, bound, and led back into Jerusalem.

The Sites Today

More than any other episode in the Bible, the events of the Passion story transpire against a definite background of time and

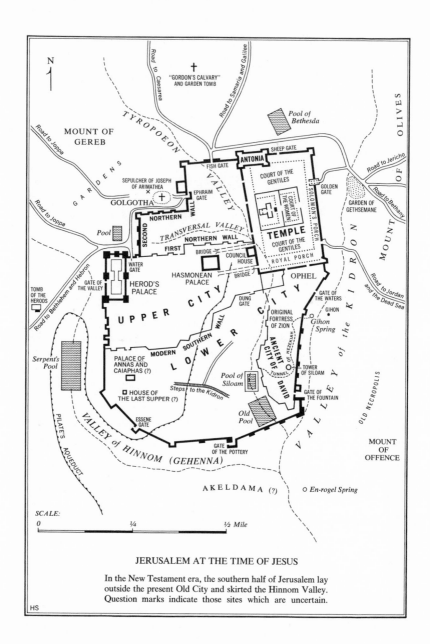

N

MOUNT OF
GEREB

"GORDON'S CALVARY"
AND GARDEN TOMB

Pool of
Bethesda

Road to Caesarea

Road to Samaria and Galilee

T Y R O P O E O N

MOUNT OF OLIVES

Road to Joppa

G A R D E N S

Road to Joppa

SEPULCHER OF JOSEPH
OF ARIMATHEA

GOLGOTHA

FISH GATE

ANTONIA

SHEEP GATE

EPHRAIM
GATE

COURT OF THE
GENTILES

COURT OF
THE WOMEN

GOLDEN
GATE

Road to Jericho

GARDEN OF
GETHSEMANE

Road to Bethany

NORTHERN
WALL

Pool

TRANSVERSAL VALLEY

NORTHERN WALL

TEMPLE

SOLOMON'S PORCH

COURT OF THE
GENTILES

M O U N T

SECOND

FIRST

BRIDGE

COUNCIL
HOUSE

ROYAL PORCH

TOMB
OF THE
HERODS

GATE OF
THE VALLEY

WATER
GATE

HEROD'S
PALACE

HASMONEAN
PALACE

BRIDGE

OPHEL

GATE OF
THE WATERS

O F   T H E   K I D R O N

Road to Bethlehem and Hebron

U P P E R   C I T Y

DUNG
GATE

ORIGINAL
FORTRESS
OF ZION

GIHON

*Gihon
Spring*

Road to Jordan
and the Dead Sea

Road to Bethlehem and Hebron

MODERN

SOUTHERN   WALL

L O W E R   C I T Y

V A L L E Y   of the

*Serpent's
Pool*

PALACE OF
ANNAS AND
CAIAPHAS (?)

HOUSE OF
THE LAST SUPPER (?)

Steps to the Kidron

Pool of
Siloam

ANCIENT
CITY OF
DAVID

HEZEKIAH'S
TUNNEL

TOWER
OF SILOAM

OLD NECROPOLIS

PILATE'S

ESSENE
GATE

GATE OF
THE FOUNTAIN

V A L L E Y   of   H I N N O M   (GEHENNA)

Old
Pool

GATE
OF THE POTTERY

MOUNT
OF
OFFENCE

AQUEDUCT

AKELDAMA (?)

○ *En-rogel Spring*

SCALE:

0   ¼   ½ Mile

JERUSALEM AT THE TIME OF JESUS

In the New Testament era, the southern half of Jerusalem lay
outside the present Old City and skirted the Hinnom Valley.
Question marks indicate those sites which are uncertain.

HS

place in one locality—Jerusalem and vicinity—so the various movements of Jesus should be traceable today. Each Holy Week, in fact, thousands of Christian pilgrims stream into Jerusalem and recapitulate the memorable events by trying to follow Jesus' footsteps from site to sacred site.

Some visitors return home disappointed, but these probably went to Palestine in the hopes of seeing Herod's Temple intact, Roman soldiers still milling about, the true cross standing at Calvary, and, if it could be scheduled, a miracle or two, if not an apostle's autograph inside a Bible.

Others criticize the somewhat drab beige landscape of the countryside, with only rare patches of verdant green. Modern Palestine, indeed, is no longer the Canaan flowing with milk and honey, thanks to several millennia of deforestation, erosion, and the root-devouring appetites of the sheep and goats who seem to own the land. And yet the topography remains essentially that of Jesus' day, though with seven to thirteen feet more altitude because the dust of centuries and the debris of conquests have settled on the land.

Today's tourist in Palestine must carefully distinguish between the authentic sites—as absolute as the River Jordan or the Sea of Galilee—such as the Mount of Olives, for example, or the location of the great Temple; probable traditional sites, as the Garden of Gethsemane; and on down to such pious but futile guesses as the "Well of the Magi," the "precise spot" where the Wise Men supposedly saw the guiding star again after they had left Jerusalem for Bethlehem!

The sites of Holy Week seem to grow with authenticity and prove more locatable as the days move on. The place where Mary and Martha lived in Bethany, for example, is not really known, nor is the exact route used by Jesus on Palm Sunday. The site for the Last Supper is hazy, but the location of Gethsemane, the high priest's palace, Pilate's praetorium, and Calvary can be pinpointed with some precision.

To be sure, today's visitor has the choice of four different

Gethsemanes, at shrines belonging to the Greek Orthodox, Latin, Armenian, and Russian Orthodox Christians. But all of these lie close to one another on the lower slopes of the Mount of Olives and above the Kidron ravine, and all might have been included in the larger olive grove that was Gethsemane. Most visitors prefer the Latin Gethsemane, where the Church of All Nations is erected over fourth-century ruins surrounding the traditional rock where Jesus prayed. Adjacent to it lies a grove in which eight ancient, gnarled olive trees, which may be 900 years old, still bear a few shriveled olives every other year.

The grove is walled in and planted with an attractive garden of flower beds. A few guides occasionally test the credulity of tourists by claiming that "these very trees witnessed Christ's suffering when they were seedlings." But even if the olive trees lived twice as long, all the ancient groves around Jerusalem were destroyed when the Roman general Titus besieged and conquered the city in 70 A.D. If, however, a botanist were asked: might such trees have grown from the root systems of olive trees standing two thousand years ago, he would have to answer Yes.

5

ANNAS AND CAIAPHAS

When day came, the assembly of the elders of the people gathered together, both chief priests and scribes; and they led him away to their council, and they said . . . "Are you the Son of God, then?" And he said to them, "You say that I am." And they said, "What further testimony do we need?"

Luke 22:66, 70–71

TRACING THE EVENTS immediately after Jesus' arrest is made somewhat difficult by the variant accounts given in the four Gospels. Their testimony may be schematized as follows, with each reporting Jesus' appearance before the priestly authorities at the following times and places:

	Matthew	*Mark*	*Luke*	*John*
Time:	Night*	Night*	Day	Night
Place:	House of Caiaphas	House of the high priest	House of the high priest	Annas, then Caiaphas

*however, with official proceedings the next morning

The issue is further complicated by both Annas and Caiaphas being called the high priest at various places in the New Testament. And yet all the accounts contribute to the total picture of the hearings and are not mutually exclusive.

Jesus was first brought by night into the southwestern Upper City to the house of Annas, who had been high priest from 6 to 15 A.D.—the pontiff in charge at the time Jesus appeared in the Temple as a young prodigy. Although deposed from that office by the Romans, Annas continued as the wealthy power-behind-the-scene in the sacerdotal aristocracy at Jerusalem, since five of

45

his own sons, and now his son-in-law Caiaphas, eventually suc-
ceeded to the high priesthood. It was not only as a mark of
respect to his authority, but possibly also in the nature of a
preliminary, lower court hearing that Jesus was first brought
before the patriarch Annas, who could still be called "high
priest," much as ex-governors today are still called Governor
So-and-so out of courtesy.

Jesus was not very cooperative before Annas, for he knew that
the major confrontation would come later before Caiaphas and
the Sanhedrin. The patriarch questioned Jesus about his followers and his teaching, but he blunted the query. "My teachings are
a matter of public record," he replied. "I taught openly in the
synagogue and in the Temple. Ask the people what I said."

One of the guards thought this attitude impertinent. "Is *that*
how you answer a high priest?" he demanded, and gave Jesus a
smart slap on the cheek.

Jesus turned to him and said, "If I spoke wrongly, produce the
evidence. But if correctly, why do you strike me?"

So ended any hopes of a preliminary hearing. Annas sent Jesus,
shackled, over to his son-in-law Caiaphas, the current high priest.
Probably the two pontiffs lived at the same palace in southwestern Jerusalem, with only a courtyard separating their apartments.

Before Caiaphas

By now it was midnight. Ordinarily, no further action would
have been taken in the case of Jesus until morning, for any proceedings involving a man's life had to take place in full daylight,
according to Jewish law. Caiaphas, however, knew that a lengthy,
daytime trial that would have attracted Jesus' popular following,
once news of his arrest broke, was extremely undesirable. It
could spark the kind of uproar that would require Pilate's troops.
Why not another nocturnal hearing now, which could hear all the
facts in the case and so facilitate a quick Sanhedral decision,
passing formal judgment, as soon as day broke on the morrow?

The prisoner would then be in Pilate's hands before the case could become a *cause célèbre*. This, in fact, is what most probably happened, which would explain New Testament references to nocturnal as well as daytime proceedings.

The chief priests and members of the council had gathered in the assembly hall of Caiaphas' palace upon urgent summons from the high priest's messengers. There could be no indictment unless at least two witnesses testified on a given charge, so Caiaphas opened the proceedings by soliciting such witnesses.

Numbers were no problem, but the testimonies were: they simply did not agree. The evidence—probably isolated acts in which Jesus had allegedly violated the Sabbath—did not jibe with the kind of precision demanded under Jewish law. In the haste of the affair, the chief priests had not had time to interview witnesses beforehand and screen out any worthless testimony.

Finally it seemed that two men could agree on a solid charge: they claimed that Jesus had said, "I am able to destroy the temple of God and rebuild it in three days." But their testimony fell apart when it was plain that Jesus referred to the "temple" of his own body.

Disgruntled at the lack of progress, Caiaphas stood up and tried for one last time the ploy of the previous days: snaring Jesus in his own words. Fixing his gaze on the defendant, he asked, "Have *you* no answer to the charges these witnesses bring against you?"

Jesus did not reply. Legally, he did not have to, since no proven evidence had yet been introduced into the proceedings.

Finally, with his case falling completely apart, Caiaphas managed to score a brilliant thrust into the very core of the issue by posing his fateful question: "I adjure you by the living God to tell us. . . . *Are you the Messiah? The Christ? Are you the Son of God?*"

A ruler of God's people had charged the question with the most solemn oath known to the Hebrews. Jesus did not try to evade it. History, quite literally, was hanging on his response. Jesus said, "I am"—this, according to Mark's version. Matthew has it, "You have said so," while Luke reads, "You say that I am."

Much has been made of the apparently indirect replies, and the slogan is often heard, "Jesus never claimed to be the Messiah." But this is not true, for all three answers are really identical. Even though the wording in Matthew and Luke may sound evasive, Jewish custom discouraged a bald Yes or No to questions of grave import. Just six hours earlier at the Last Supper, Jesus had also replied to Judas' question, "Is it I?" with a sad, "You have said so" (Mt. 26:25).

Underlining his categorical claim to Messiahship, Jesus added, "Hereafter you will see the Son of man sitting at the right hand of the power of God."

Tearing his high priestly robe "the length of the palm of the hand"—the inches required when blasphemy was heard—Caiaphas struggled to be heard above the rising commotion. *"Blasphemy!"* he cried. "Do we need any further witnesses? You have heard his blasphemy: *you* are now the witnesses!—What is your finding?"

A chorus of voices offered a unanimous opinion: "He deserves death."

But was it really blasphemy? Jesus' claim to be Messiah was either true or false, and should have been examined in detail by Caiaphas. But even if it were proven false, the claim itself was not necessarily blasphemous. According to the Talmud, blasphemy technically occurred only when the sacred name of God as he revealed it to Moses—Yahweh—was uttered. Whether or not Jesus used it is not known, since the Gospels were written in Greek, but it seems he did not.

The entire hearing, however, had violated so many other provisions in Jewish law that no technicality at this point could stand in the way of the high priest's virtually directed verdict of Guilty in a surcharged emotional atmosphere. Some scholars have questioned the accuracy of the New Testament in this section: a hearing with so many violations could never have occurred, they claim. Since our information on standard Jewish legal procedure comes from the Talmud, compiled two or three centuries after Christ, there is no absolute proof that all the same legal usage applied then. Yet, even if it did, everything we know about Annas, Caiaphas, and the clan would lead to the conclusion that in the present emergency the end would easily justify the means in their estimation.

Is this being too hard on the chief priests? Apparently not. Some very negative opinions about the high priestly family appear also in Jewish traditions. "Woe to the family of Annas! Woe to their serpent-like hisses!" warns the Talmud, while Josephus styles Annas' son Ananus as "very insolent."

Peter's Denial

In this section of the Passion history, there is a tug of war for the reader's attention between the dramatic scene unfolding inside the high priest's palace and the incredible performance of Peter standing outside in the courtyard, warming himself before a charcoal fire flaming in a brazier. At the beginning of April, nights are still cool in Jerusalem, and the Passover moon was offering no warmth whatever.

Of the disciples who fled from Gethsemane, nine continued in hiding, but two of them—John and Peter—cautiously followed Jesus at some distance. John, who evidently had some friends among the high priest's staff, was able to gain their admittance inside the palace. While Peter was warming himself before the fire—and unintentionally illuminating his face—a doormaid came up to him and challenged, "Weren't you also with Jesus the Galilean?"

Before Peter could even think about it, the lie was out. "I don't know what you're talking about, woman," he snapped.

Later on came a more serious challenge. A relative of Malchus, the servant whose ear Peter had removed, sauntered over to him and said, "Didn't I see you out in the garden with him?"

"Man, I don't know what you mean." Was that straining, high-

Israel Ministry of Tourism, Jerusalem

Aerial view looking eastward across the Old City of Jerusalem, with identifications on the opposite page numbering Jesus' final movements on Maundy Thursday and Good Friday. The early morning meeting of the Sanhedrin likely took place at the Council House on the Temple mount (3), while Pontius Pilate had his tribunal at the Palace of Herod (4, 6), the site of which is now occupied by the Citadel. Jesus' appearance

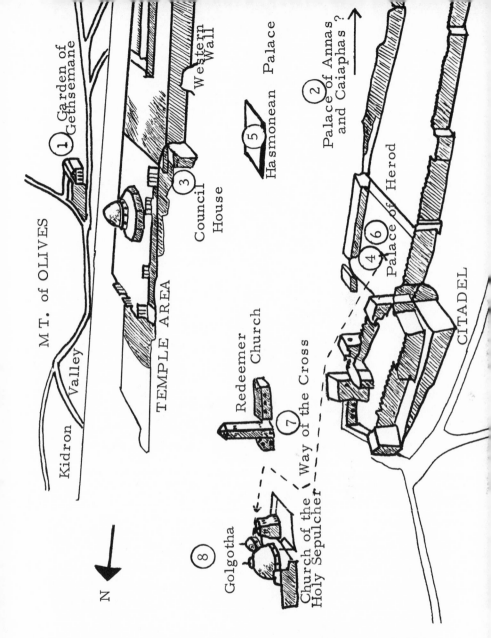

MT. of OLIVES

Kidron Valley

① Garden of Gethsemane

Western Wall

TEMPLE AREA

③ Council House

⑤ Hasmonean Palace

Palace of Annas and Caiaphas ?

② Palace of Annas and Caiaphas ?

Palace of Herod

④ ⑥

CITADEL

N

⑧ Golgotha

Redeemer Church

⑦ Way of the Cross

Church of the Holy Sepulcher

before Herod Antipas took place at the Hasmonean Palace (5), of which nothing remains today. The route to Golgotha, indicated in (7), is *far* more likely than the traditional Via Dolorosa, which leads from the northwestern end of the Temple area westward to Golgotha (8). The Western Wall of the Temple mount is sometimes called the "Wailing Wall."

Bronze

Obv. Lituus; inscription: ΤΙΒΕΡΙΟΥ ΚΑΙCΑΡΟC
(Tiberius Caesar).
Rev. Within a wreath, the date: L ΙΖ (17=A.D.
30/31).

Roman denar, silver; tribute money

Obv. Head of Tiberius; inscription: TI CAESAR
DIVI AUG F AUGUSTUS (Tiberius Caesar, son
of the divine Augustus, Augustus).
Rev. Pax seated, holding branch; inscription:
PONTIF MAXIM (High priest).

Syrian tetradrachma, silver

Obv. Head of Augustus; inscription: ΚΑΙΣΑΡΟΣ
ΣΕΒΑΣΤΟΣ (Caesar, Augustus).
Rev. Tyche of Antiochia; at his feet, the river-god
Orontes; inscription: ΑΝΤΙΟΧΕΩΝ ΜΗΤΡΟ-
ΠΟΛΕΩΣ (Capital of the Antiochian); date: ΔΝ
(54; after Pharsalus), ςϚ Λ (36 after Actium=
A.D. 5).

The Interpreter's Dictionary of the Bible, © *1962, Abingdon Press*

The thirty pieces of silver paid to Judas were most probably thirty she-
kels coined in Tyre or Antioch, a specimen of which is the Syrian tetradrachma at the bottom of the illustration above. The tribute money
shown to Jesus in the famous "Render to Caesar" confrontation is in the
center, while a coin minted by Pontius Pilate in Judea is shown above.

pitched sound a cock crowing? Peter may not have noticed it—yet.

An hour later, when he finally thought himself wrapped in a cozy blanket of anonymity, somebody made fun of Peter's Galilean twang. It was a standing joke that you couldn't tell if a Galilean were talking about an ass, a lamb, or a jug of wine, since they pronounced *hamor, immar,* and *hamar* just about the same. "Certainly you're one of them," he sneered, "since even your speech betrays you."

Like a caged animal prodded by tormentors, Peter furiously lashed back at his accusers, adding curses and swearing to emphasize his denials. This time he heard the cock crow distinctly, piercingly. Tears in his eyes, he dragged himself out of the courtyard and indulged his private remorse.

Jesus, meanwhile, was abandoned to the whims of the Temple guard. While being led to the cell where he would spend the few remaining hours of the night, he suffered the indignities and abuses common in ancient prisons each time the authorities turned the other way. He was blindfolded and subjected to jeers, spittle, slaps, and blows. "Now prophesy for us, Jesus," they screamed, "who hit you?"

A hopeless prophet! He wasn't saying a thing.

The Sanhedrin Convenes

At dawn the next morning, Jesus was brought before an official session of the Great Sanhedrin, which had convened on the Temple mount. After bare formalities, which included asking Jesus the momentous question once more and getting his reply, Caiaphas again requested a verdict from the Sanhedrists. Since many of the members had already spent much of the night at the high priest's palace during the previous conclave, their action merely served to ratify what they had already decided.

Attention now focused on the youngest of the seventy members of the Sanhedrin, who was seated at the edge of the semicircle of benches. According to custom, the voting would begin with him—lest he be influenced by his superiors—and end with the eldest member, the high priest casting the final vote. The youthful Sanhedrist stood up in the hushed chamber and said, "He is worthy of death."

The next member arose and said the same. Whispering in the hall rose steadily as the count continued, "Guilty," "Death."

The final tally—if all members were present—would probably have been 69 votes for condemnation and 2 abstentions. These came from Sanhedrists named Joseph of Arimathea and Nicodemus, who were secret followers of Jesus.

If Judea were not a Roman province, Jesus would now have been executed by stoning, probably below the east wall of Jerusalem. But the *jus gladii,* the "law of the sword"—the right to execute capital punishment—was now reserved for the Roman prefect of Judea, Pontius Pilate, who would have to review the Sanhedrin's verdict and pronounce sentence or dismiss the case.

A brief, tragic note closes this phase of the story. Too late and too pathetically, Judas suffered his pangs of remorse. With a desperate but honest naïveté, he appeared at the Temple, clutching a bag with thirty unspent pieces of silver chinking inside. "I have sinned in betraying innocent blood," he said, handing the priests the bag as if to buy back Jesus' freedom. However ingenuous, it was the last right thing Judas ever did.

"What is that to us?" the priests replied. "See to it yourself."

Throwing the coins onto the marble floor of the Temple, Judas hurried out of the sacred precincts in total despair. Finding a rope and a convenient tree standing just under the south wall of the city, he hung himself. And this at a time when, in Christian theology, Jesus would literally be dying to forgive him.

Later, the priests took the money and bought a small plot with it in which to bury Judas and other strangers. The so-called "Field of Blood" is still shown south of Jerusalem on the other side of the Hinnom Valley. But any precision in such a matter, of course, is impossible.

6

PONTIUS PILATE

Now Jesus stood before the governor; and the governor asked him,
"Are you the King of the Jews?" Jesus said to him, "You have said so."

MATTHEW 27:11

DURING THE SMOLDERING SUMMER of 1961, some Italian archae-
ologists were excavating an ancient theater at Caesarea, the
Mediterranean port that served as the Roman capital of Palestine,
when they unearthed a two-by-three-foot stone that bore some
kind of inscription. Antonio Frova, who was in charge of the dig,
cleaned out the lettering with a brush, and suddenly his eyes
widened in disbelief while his face was cut by a vast grin. The left
third of the inscription had been chipped away, but Frova reconstructed it in short order. The following Latin had originally been
cut into the stone in three-inch lettering:

CAESARIENS. TIBERIÉVM
PONTIVS PILATVS
PRAEFECTVS IVDAEAE
DÈDIT

"Pontius Pilatus, Prefect of Judea, has presented the Tiberiéum
to the Caesareans." The Tiberiéum, evidently, was some kind of
public structure named in honor of the Roman emperor
Tiberius.

This simple but proud sentence marked the first archaeological
evidence for the existence of Pontius Pilate ever to be discovered,
and it added dramatically to our knowledge about one of the
most fascinating yet enigmatic figures from the past. His name is

repeated every moment at Masses being conducted across the world, and each Sunday by nearly a billion Christians as they recite the words of the Creed. In that sense, he is easily the most famous Roman of them all, for many who know little about a Caesar or Augustus or even Nero still confess the words, "I believe in Jesus Christ . . . who . . . suffered under Pontius Pilate."

Surprisingly, Pilate is termed Prefect of Judea in this inscription. Under the entry "Pontius Pilate" in nearly every encyclopedia or reference work on the Bible, the Roman is invariably styled a procurator, a mistaken term based on what has now proven to be anachronisms by the first historians who refer to Pilate. It was only later, under the emperor Claudius, that the title of Roman governors of Judea shifted to procurator. The Roman prefect had more military responsibilities than the procurator, and the New Testament very accurately labels Pilate as governor, not procurator.

Hardly due to any personal achievement, Pontius Pilate became the pin in a hinge of destiny simply because he presided at a trial that would become one of the central events in history. Aside from the Caesarea inscription, a more accurate portrait of Pilate can be drawn also from a careful rereading of the historical sources.

His very name provides two valuable hints as to his background and ancestry. Pontius, the family name, was that of a prominent clan among the Samnites, hill cousins of the Latin Romans who lived along the Apennine mountain spine southeast of Rome. A scrappy breed, the Samnites had almost conquered Rome in several fierce wars. The Pontii were of noble blood, but when Rome finally absorbed the Samnites, their aristocracy was demoted to the Roman equestrian or middle-class order.

But it is Pilate's personal name Pilatus that proves almost conclusively that he was indeed of Samnite origin. Pilatus means "Armed-with-a-javelin." The *pilum* or javelin was a balanced missile six feet long, half wooden handle and half pointed iron shaft, which Samnite mountaineers hurled at their enemies with devas-

A two-by-three-foot stone discovered at Caesarea in 1961, the first epigraphic evidence of Pontius Pilate ever found. The left facing of the stone had been chipped away for reuse, so that only "TIVSPILATVS" remains of Pilate's name in the middle line. This stone is now in the Israel Museum at Jerusalem.

tating effect. The Romans quickly copied the weapon, and it was the *pilum*, in fact, that had made the Roman Empire possible.

Roman versus Jew

Pilate ruled as prefect of Judea from 26 to 36 A.D., the second longest tenure of any first-century Roman governor in Palestine. The very length of his office contradicts the usual impression of Pilate as an incompetent official, for it is doubtful that the emperor Tiberius, who insisted on good provincial administration, would have retained Pilate in office so long had he been the political cripple of popular repute. Nor was the prefecture of Judea a petty post staffed by dissatisfied officials, an impression almost universal among Biblical novelists: in that case, Pilate need never have accepted the office.

He did, however, find the governorship of Judea a most taxing experience, and several vignettes of Pilate show the remarkably "modern" problems an ancient administrator had to face. Aside from his familiar role on Good Friday, there are five other incidents involving Pilate that are reported by the first-century authors Josephus and Philo. Because it seems that Pilate blundered in each of these instances, he has been roundly faulted for his performance as governor in most histories since that time. Yet a close study of these episodes would suggest that Pilate, while hardly a master of diplomacy, was at least trying to make the best of very difficult administrative situations.

In what came to be called "the affair of the Roman standards," Pilate's troops once marched into Jerusalem carrying medallions with the emperor's image or bust among their regimental standards. This action provoked a five-day mass demonstration by Jews at the provincial capital, Caesarea, which protested the effigies as a violation of Jewish law concerning engraved images (Ex. 20:4–5). Pilate finally relented and ordered the offensive standards removed.

Later in his administration, he built an aqueduct from cisterns near Bethlehem to improve Jerusalem's water supply, but paid for it with funds from the Temple treasury. This sparked another riot, which was put down only after bloodshed, even though Pilate had cautioned his troops not to use swords.

While this seems a grotesque example of malfeasance, a case could be made that Jewish sacred writings permitted expenditure of surplus Temple funds for such civic needs as water supply, and it would seem that Pilate must have had some cooperation from priestly authorities in Jerusalem. He could not simply have plundered the sacrosanct Temple treasury: gentiles were forbidden, on pain of death, to enter the Temple interior, where the sacred treasure was stored. Any such violation would have led to Pilate's immediate recall. And since the aqueduct fed cisterns below the Temple, building operations could hardly have been undertaken in that area without at least tacit approval of the religious authorities. Apparently, the subsequent outcry was a protest of the people, not their leaders, who may even have warned Pilate in advance of the approaching demonstration.

On another occasion, Pilate set up several golden shields in his Jerusalem headquarters that, unlike the standards, bore no images whatever, only a bare inscription of dedication to Tiberius. And yet the people protested even the imageless shields, but this time Pilate refused to remove them. He could, and perhaps did, point to the precedent of Jews in Alexandria, who adorned the very walls of their synagogues with gilded shields in honor of the Roman emperor. But Alexandria was not Jerusalem, and the Judeans formally protested to Tiberius. In a very testy letter, the emperor ordered Pilate to transfer the shields to a temple in Caesarea, and ominously warned him to uphold all the religious and political customs of his Jewish subjects.

It was only a few months after this bizarre affair that Pilate made his entry on the stage of history as judge of Jesus of Nazareth, and the episode of the golden shields *is critically important in understanding Pilate's conduct at the trial,* as will be noted in the next chapter. Indeed, the Roman viewpoint in the "greatest

Prof. Avi-Yonah's model of the Palace of Herod in western Jerusalem, where Jesus stood before Pontius Pilate. The two wings of the palace within the fortified enclave were named the Caesareum and the Agrippeum, for Herod the Great's Roman friends. The three large towers guarding the northern end were called *(l* to *r)*: Phasael, Hippicus, and Mariamne. In the upper right stand the four towers of the Fortress Antonia, looming over the Temple area just off the picture to the right.

story ever told" has been remarkably neglected, and yet it offers an important key to understanding the events of Holy Week.

The episode of the golden shields also provides a valuable (and strangely overlooked) clue as to where Jesus stood before Pilate on Good Friday. The traditional location shown to most visitors in Jerusalem—the ancient pavement of the Tower Antonia northwest of the Temple area and now under the Sisters of Zion convent—seems erroneous, even if it is the starting point of the Via Dolorosa, the "Sorrowful Road" along which a mournful parade of Christians passes each Good Friday. Rather, the Jewish philosopher Philo, who recorded the episode of the golden shields, wrote that Pilate hung the shields "in Herod's palace in the holy city," which he further identified as "the house of the governors." The lavish palace constructed by Herod the Great on the western edge of old Jerusalem was indeed preferable to the Spartan accommodations at the Antonia fortress, and Jesus' trial undoubtedly took place there.

It is further unlikely that Pilate's wife, Procula, who accompanied him to Jerusalem that fateful week, would have been subjected to quarters in a military barracks. The New Testament merely says that the trial took place at Pilate's praetorium, which was anywhere a Roman magistrate decided to hold court. But as late as 66 A.D., the Roman governor Gessius Florus was still setting up his tribunal just outside Herod's palace, according to the Jewish historian Josephus, *exactly as Pilate did.* The evidence, then, would seem conclusive.

Judging the Judge

Finishing Pilate's story, however, takes us to events three years after Good Friday. Strangely, it was no imbroglio with his Jewish subjects that ended Pilate's term in Judea but rather a furore involving Samaritans, those half-breed cousins of the Jews who lived in mid-Palestine. An obscure pseudo-prophet with Messianic ambitions promised the Samaritans that he would uncover some sacred temple utensils that Moses had supposedly buried on their sacred Mt. Gerizim, and a host of credulous Samaritans gathered to witness the spectacle. Because the multitude had come armed with weapons—perhaps also to prevent the people from being exploited—Pilate ordered his troops to block the route of ascent. It came to a pitched battle. Pilate's forces won, and the leaders of the uprising were executed. Here again, Pilate's action, while certainly harsh, was not more than what other Roman governors had done under similar circumstances to subdue what had developed into armed sedition astride the main artery of Palestine.

The Samaritan Senate, however, complained to Pilate's superior, the proconsul of Syria, who ordered Pilate to return to Rome to answer the charges against him. With no choice in the matter, Pilate departed for Rome late in 36. Was Judge Pontius Pilate himself judged in Rome? Probably we shall never know. Josephus' record, our principal source, breaks off with this intriguing sentence: "But before he reached Rome, Tiberius had already died." Gaius Caligula, the successor emperor, either heard Pilate's case or, more probably, quashed it, as he did most of the cases carried over from Tiberius' administration.

The traditional view of Pilate's fate, however, is extremely negative. Although early Christianity intended the wording of the Creed ("suffered under Pontius Pilate") merely to document the event and not necessarily to assign guilt, the blame developed anyway, and for the last seventeen centuries Pilate has had an unusually bad press. The most terrifying—and certainly imaginative—punishments were invented for him: torture, insanity, exile, compulsive handwashing, suicide, drowning, decapitation, being swallowed by the earth, and even that ancient punishment for parricide: being sewn up in an ox-hide with a cock, a viper, and a monkey, and pitched into a river. Medieval legends would add tales of his restless corpse, accompanied by squadrons of demons, disrupting localities from France to Switzerland, causing storms, earthquakes, and other havoc.

On the basis of the earliest sources, however, it is clear that nothing of the sort ever happened to Pilate, let alone to his corpse. Although the tradition of Pilate's suicide dates back to the fourth-century church historian Eusebius, there are difficulties in his evidence. And the more important testimony of the earlier church father Origen, plus conclusions from first-century historians, decidedly contradict the suicide story. Nothing grossly negative, it seems, ever befell Pilate.

What, then, did happen to him? Much later Lenten preaching to the contrary, the early church father Tertullian claimed that Pilate "was a Christian in his conscience." Greek Orthodoxy canonized his wife, while the Ethiopian church even recognizes a St. Pilate and St. Procula's Day on June 25. Saint or sinner, Pilate most probably spent the rest of his days as a retired government official, a pensioned Roman magistrate emeritus, enjoying a less than sensational fate. He may even have spent his time looking for an answer to the question he once asked, under circumstances he may well have forgotten, "What is truth?"

Yet all this lay in the distant future. When he arose early Friday morning on April 3, 33 A.D., Pontius Pilate could hear no drum roll of destiny as he prepared to adjudicate the cases waiting at his tribunal. But his appointment with history was waiting for him in the person of a manacled prisoner being brought into the paved esplanade in front of Herod's palace by a huge throng.

1. The city of Jerusalem from the Mount of Olives. Above the slopes descending to the Kidron Valley stands the golden Dome of the Rock, constructed over the site of the great Herodian and Solomonic temples. The walled platform surrounding this area still contains Herodian masonry.

2. The Mount of Olives with the Church of All Nations in the foreground, sheltering olive trees at the reputed site for the Garden of Gethsemane. Onion domes in the upper right mark the Russian Orthodox Church of St. Mary Magdalene. The pathway to the left may have been used by Jesus on Palm Sunday.

3. A first-century, rock-hewn Jewish sepulcher at Abu-Gosh, west of Jerusalem, similar to the one in which Jesus was buried.

4. One of the towers of the Citadel in western Jerusalem, whose lower half shows surviving Herodian masonry that once constituted the base of the Tower Phasael, the largest of the three towers at the northern end of the Palace of Herod. Since Roman governors of Judea regularly held court in this palace, these great blocks of stone undoubtedly witnessed Jesus' condemnation by Pontius Pilate.

4

5. The westernmost bulge of the Sea of Galilee where Magdala was located, home of Mary Magdalene. The Gospels record several resurrection appearances of Jesus in this vicinity, including the fish breakfast on the shores of the Sea (John 21) and the mountain appearance (Matthew 28), traditionally associated with the hills around Safad on the peak to the right.

7

A ROMAN TRIAL

And the chief priests accused him of many things. And Pilate again asked him, "Have you no answer to make? See how many charges they bring against you." But Jesus made no further answer, so that Pilate wondered.

MARK 15:3–5

UNDOUBTEDLY, PILATE HAD SOME ADVANCE notice from Caiaphas that the case of Jesus of Nazareth would be coming before his tribunal. The governor ordered his ivory *sella curulis,* the magistrate's official chair, moved outside the palace to a raised dais overlooking the plaza to the east, which had filled with a vast multitude. This was to accommodate the people, who would have defiled themselves for the Passover Seder that night had they entered a pagan headquarters.

Turning to the prosecution, Pilate asked, in common Hellenistic Greek, "What charge do you bring against this man?" It was the opening formula for a Roman trial, the *interrogatio.*

Several of the chief priests, who were acting as principal *accusatores* or prosecutors, presented a formal bill of indictment: "We found this man subverting our nation, forbidding the payment of tribute money to Tiberius Caesar, and claiming that he is Messiah, a king." The charges were superbly tailored to alarm a Roman governor, for they fairly glowed with sedition and treason. Of the religious grounds on which Jesus had been condemned by the Sanhedrin there was not a word, since the priestly authorities knew that Pilate could hardly put a man to death for the purely theological offense of blasphemy.

Since no one seemed ready to defend Jesus, Pilate thought it fair to give him a brief, confidential hearing before proceeding with the trial in order to learn something more about the defendant apart from the glare of his accusers. Summoning Jesus inside the palace, he inquired, *"Are* you the king of the Jews?" In other words, "How do you plead?"

Jesus looked up at him, his face showing the abuse of the past hours and the lack of sleep. "Do you ask this of your own accord," he replied, "or did others tell it to you concerning me?"

"What! Am I a Jew? Your own nation and the chief priests have brought you before me. What have you done?"

"My kingship is not of this world. If it were, my followers would fight to defend me. But my authority as king comes from elsewhere."

"So? You *are* a king, then?"

"It is as you say, that I am a king. For this I was born, and for this I have come into the world: to bear witness to the truth. Everyone who is of the truth hears my voice."

"A kingship of *truth,* you say?" Pilate wondered. "What *is* truth?"

Evidently the private hearing convinced Pilate that Jesus' claims for kingship—his visionary "kingship of truth"—had no political implications, so it would hardly be possible to construct a case of treason against him. Ordering the defendant back to his outdoor tribunal, Pilate announced, "I find no case against Jesus thus far. What evidence do you have to substantiate your charges?"

Now far better organized than at the Sanhedral hearing, the prosecution chose its witnesses well, who made much of Jesus' Messianic claims and probably added new evidence, such as Jesus' violence in the Temple. According to early sources outside the New Testament, there may also have been testimony indicting Jesus for magic and sorcery in the case of so-called miracles.

When the prosecution rested its case, Pilate turned to Jesus, who had remained silent the whole time, and asked, "Have you *nothing* to say in your own defense? Don't you hear all this evidence against you?"

Jesus said not a word, supplying no defense of any kind, not even to a single charge. Pilate was astonished at his conduct, and probably asked the crowd, "Can anyone offer evidence favoring the defendant, Jesus of Nazareth?"—for so he would have been obliged under Roman law.

Whatever response there may have been, it was hopelessly submerged by calls for condemnation from the multitude. Most of the vast throng, which was composed of the priestly establishment as well as the staff, police, and servant corps of the Temple, had marched directly westward from the Temple to Herod's palace, and they were starting to get restless. The prosecution now enlarged on Jesus' alleged sedition: "His teachings are inflaming the people throughout all Judea, starting from Galilee and spreading even as far as this city."

"Beginning in Galilee?" Pilate wondered. "Is the defendant a Galilean?"

The *accusatores* happily confirmed that Jesus grew up in Galilee and recently lived in Capernaum, for Galileans had a reputation for rebellion and this could undergird their indictment.

But Pilate had other ideas in mind with this information. Stated simply, he wanted to unload this troublesome case that was really religious and not political in essence. Yes, he had likely heard how Jesus had roasted the Temple aristocracy in his preaching, but there had been no intelligence on Jesus' supposed political treason. So now he announced, "The defendant, then, is clearly a Galilean, and, as such, he is under the authority of the tetrarch Herod Antipas. And since Herod is in Jerusalem at this very moment, I think it eminently proper to remand this case to his jurisdiction."

Waving aside all protests, Pilate invoked what would later be called change of venue and sent Jesus under armed guard to the Hasmonean palace, which lay due east about two-thirds of the distance back to the Temple, for this is where Herod Antipas and his entourage were staying at the time. Legally, Pilate *did* have the authority to try Jesus in Judea as the *forum delicti* of his alleged crime, the place of the offense. But he also had the option of remanding the case to the jurisdiction of the sovereign of the accused, since Galilee was his *forum domicilii*, the place of residence. And since the tetrarch understood Jewish religious law better than he did, the shift was logical enough.

Before Herod Antipas

The tetrarch—"ruler of a quarter (of Palestine)"—was one of the sons of Herod the Great, the Temple builder and king of the Christmas story, and his domain included Galilee, as well as lands east of the Dead Sea. His brother Archelaus had originally ruled Judea, but he had made such a mess of it that Rome exiled him in 6 A.D. and then dispatched a series of her governors to rule Judea, the latest of whom was Pilate.

There was, then, divided authority in Palestine, and the ambitious Antipas had brutally embarrassed Pilate by forwarding a letter of protest over his head to the emperor in the case of the golden shields. Since this episode had virtually placed Pilate on probation, he thought an olive branch waved in Herod's direction might be more suitable than revenge for the moment, and sending Jesus to his tribunal would be an unmistakable courtesy. In fact, it was the second reason for the change of venue.

Herod Antipas could not have been more pleased. For many months he had wanted to meet Jesus, that miracle-worker about whom tongues were wagging across the land. It was getting almost embarrassing: a native of Galilee was supposedly performing wonders and yet the ruler of Galilee had never seen any! Herod eyed the prisoner with obvious interest, and then must have said something like, "Do a miracle, Jesus."

The prisoner did nothing, said nothing. He would stage no

spectacle for the man who had beheaded his close friend, fore-runner, and cousin, John the Baptizer. He would not entertain the sly opportunist whom he had once called "That Fox"; nor his painted wife, Herodias, who had previously been married to his brother; nor her dancing daughter Salome, who was proba-bly also in Jerusalem for the annual Herodian family Passover reunion.

The priestly prosecution repeated its formal indictment against Jesus, but this time they did not demur at introducing also the religious issues that had led to Jesus' conviction before the Sanhedrin, since Herod had very nobly led their complaint against Pilate in the case of the golden shields. Certainly in an issue of much greater significance, he would support them once again.

Herod prodded Jesus for some reaction, but got nothing. Em-barrassed and at the limit of his patience, he invited his troops to wade in for a round of derision and contempt. Dressing Jesus in a brilliant white robe—the Messiah was expected to wear such —they performed their mock reverence.

"All right, that's enough," Herod must finally have directed. "Now take this magnificent prophet-Messiah-monarch back to Pontius Pilate."

Even though Luke makes no reference to it, the prosecution must have felt bitterly betrayed by Herod Antipas. They had expected easy cooperation, an ideal shortcut to their goal, but now it had eluded them. The tetrarch's motives, however, were obvious: he was still enduring the popular odium for having killed one prophet—John—so he would not tackle a second, especially when his chief steward, Chuza, and his adviser Manaen were followers of the Nazarene, not to mention numerous of his Galilean subjects. But it was very decent of Pilate to make such a conciliatory gesture, and so, as Luke puts it, "Herod and Pilate became friends with each other that very day, for before this they had been at enmity with each other" (23:12).

Back to Pilate

The return of the prisoner to his jurisdiction was a bitter, though not unexpected, surprise for Pilate. But perhaps he could use it as an excuse to quash the case. Seizing the initiative, he announced, "You brought the defendant before this tribunal on a charge of subverting the people. But after examining him before you, I did not find him guilty of any of your prime charges. Neither did the tetrarch Herod Antipas, for he has referred the case back to us. I will therefore chastise him and release him, since he has done nothing to deserve death."

This provoked a general outcry from the crowd for the first time, a rising rumble of disapproval punctuated by shouts of "Away with him! Crucify him!"

The rest of the story is painfully familiar: Pilate lamely tried to offer the multitude a choice between Passover amnesty for Jesus or the insurrectionary Bar-Abbas, assuming they would easily choose Jesus—but they surprised him. Next, Pilate's wife added an ominous overtone with her famous note: "Have nothing to do with that righteous man, for I have suffered much over him today in a dream" (Mt. 27:19). A modern might dismiss this as a housewifely intrusion with bad timing, but dreams were very important to the Romans, for they were thought to predict future events. Everyone knew about Calpurnia's dream of Caesar's torn and bloodied toga on the eve of the Ides of March.

Amid further shouts for the death sentence, Pilate had Jesus brought inside the palace courtyard for scourging. Troops gathered around the prisoner, stripped him, and then administered a brutal flogging that, Pilate hoped, might yet win the people's sympathy for the accused. Playing on the idea that this wretch should be a king in general, and *of the Jews* in particular, the anti-Semitic troops laughingly planted a crown of thorns on his head and shoved a reed into his right hand as a scepter, then did him mock homage.

When the trial of Jesus was transferred to the tribunal of Herod Antipas, Jesus was led eastward to the Hasmonean Palace, where Herod was staying at the time. This palace, reconstructed in the model at the Holy-land Hotel, is at the upper left, the building crowned by the columned twin towers. Across the center is the bridge or viaduct erected by Herod the Great to span the Tyropoeon ("Cheesemakers'") Valley separating the Temple from the rest of Jerusalem, and in the foreground stands the hippodrome or stadium built by Herod the Great for chariot races.

Pilate halted the fun and brought Jesus back before the multitude. Surely it had been punishment enough. "Behold the man!" he said, in a tone of condescending compassion.

"CRUCIFY! CRUCIFY HIM!" the shouts returned.

Pilate lost his patience. "*You* crucify him, then," he snarled, "for I've found no case against him." He now decided to close the trial.

It was then that the prosecution shifted the charges back to religious grounds, since they were making no headway on the political. "We have a law," said their spokesman, "and according to our law this man ought to die, because he has claimed to be the Son of God."

Disturbed, irritated at the new charge, and perhaps a little superstitious, Pilate drew Jesus back inside the palace for a second private hearing. He led off with a frankly metaphysical question, "Where have you come from?"

Jesus made no reply.

"You won't speak to me? Don't you know that I have the authority to release you or to crucify you?"

"You would have no authority whatever over me if it had not been given you from above," Jesus replied. "Therefore the prosecution has the greater sin."

Pilate now returned to his tribunal outside, declared Jesus not guilty, and was on the point of releasing him when, in understandable desperation, the prosecution played its trump card. Perhaps it was Caiaphas himself who said, "If you release this man, you are *not* a Friend of Caesar. For anyone who would make himself a king *treasonably* defies Caesar!"

It was a brilliant thrust that hit the mark cleanly, directly. Implied was every syllable of the following: "If you set this man free, we will send a delegation to Tiberius Caesar, accusing you of condoning treason in one who would set himself up as subversive counter-king to Rome, and also of failure to uphold our religious law. You recall Tiberius' threatening letter to you five months ago: if he upheld us then in the case of the golden shields, he'll uphold us now in a far more serious matter. You, Pilate, will have to leave your exclusive club of the Friends of Caesar. Your golden membership ring with Tiberius' image will be pulled from your fingers and you will make your exit via the usual means for disgraced members: exile, or compulsory suicide."

The club existed. High officials in the Empire and some members of the Senate were privileged to join the elite fraternity of *Amici Caesaris*, the Friends of Caesar, and no one left it except under mortal disgrace. Pilate's resistance crumbled: it was Jesus or himself, and he opted for self. His final feeble attempts to defend Jesus and the bowl in which he tried to wash his hands from responsibility in the matter were all retreating actions in the face of the mounting riot conditions that rattled cries of "Away with him! Crucify him!" across the plaza. The trial was over—also for the judge.

Drying his hands, Pilate gestured toward Jesus and said, *"Staurotheto"* to a centurion of the Jerusalem cohort. "Let him be crucified."

The Question of Responsibility

Except for the last sentence, most of the above *never happened* —according to a flurry of recent books on the life of Jesus, some by pseudo-scholars but others by very serious Biblical specialists. Despite a dozen different interpretations of Jesus' arrest and trial, they agree on two basic hypotheses: 1) that Jesus *was* indeed some sort of political revolutionary, perhaps even a Zealot, and Pilate really *wanted* to crucify so dangerous a rebel; and 2) that the New Testament documents have falsely shifted the moral responsibility for Jesus' death from Pilate to the Jewish Sanhedrin. Some scholars fault the Gospel writers for outright anti-Semitism in reporting the events of Holy Week as they did, while others suggest they were merely tampering with the truth for political reasons: unless a reluctant Pilate were made to appear pressured by Jewish authorities, how else could Romans be converted to believe in someone who was crucified by a Roman governor?

If these two hypotheses are true, then, of course, a very serious question mark is superimposed over the entire New Testament so far as its historicity, and even veracity, is concerned. But these theses have not been proven, and can very nearly be disproven. No firm link between Jesus and the Zealots has ever been established aside from the fact that one of his disciples, Simon Zelotes, had evidently been related to the movement at one time. Once, in symbolic fulfillment of prophecy, Jesus did suggest that his disciples buy swords, but when two were produced, he termed that armament program "enough" (Lk. 22:36 ff.). In any case, two swords are certainly a minuscule arsenal, and Jesus' later advice to Peter to sheathe one of them—"for those who take the sword will perish by the sword"—is hardly the remark of a political revolutionary.

The second thesis, that the Gospels falsely portray a Jewish prosecution, is far more serious. However, there is a very important, yet little known, support for the New Testament accounts from a surprising source: even purely Jewish rabbinical sources and traditions require the death penalty for Jesus of Nazareth, such as *Sanhedrin* 43a of the Babylonian Talmud, which states that he "shall be stoned because he has practiced sorcery and enticed Israel to apostasy." And almost all scholars agree that in 62 A.D., only 29 years after Good Friday, a stunning near-parallel occurred: the high priest and the Sanhedrin in Jerusalem stoned to death James, the brother (or relative) of Jesus and first Christian bishop of Jerusalem in the *absence* of the Roman governor Albinus, who was later so angry at this execution that the high priest was deposed.

The Talmud, moreover, heartily agrees with the New Testament in its evaluation of Annas and the sacerdotal aristocracy of Jerusalem in the time of Jesus. Early Jewish traditions about Jesus were later gathered also in a fifth-century compilation called the *Toledoth Jeshu,* which freely assigns all responsibility for Jesus' conviction to the priests, hardly even mentioning Pontius Pilate. And finally, long before it supposedly became necessary to "sweeten" Pilate's role on Good Friday in order to gain Roman converts, Paul was writing the same version of the events at Jerusalem in his epistles as would the Gospels later on. Unless these and similar facts are refuted by hard evidence—not the flimsies of sensational theory—the New Testament records of the trial and conviction must stand as historical in essence.

Who, then, *was* responsible for crucifying Jesus? An incredible amount of bad thinking has gone into answering this vexed query, with very tragic consequences. Obviously Pilate had the final responsibility for executing sentence, but he could very well have been pressured into it, as the Gospels claim. Were the Jews, then, morally responsible? The priestly prosecution, yes. Other Jews, too, then and since? Categorically *no!* Medieval Christianity erred tragically in developing an anti-Semitic attitude from Jewish involvement in Jesus' trial, which must stand as one of the supreme instances of illogic in Western history.

The prosecution, acting in good faith, did believe Jesus a dangerous religious errorist and possible seditionist, but that prosecution represented only a small fraction of the Jewish populace at the time, and their specific responsibility is *not* transferrable. And in view of the fact that the founder and early membership of Christianity was Jewish, and that many of his own countrymen did indeed sympathize with Jesus, it is clearly ridiculous to pin any collective responsibility for Good Friday on "the Jews" then or since. If some bigot wishes to make much of the people's famous challenge, "His blood be on us and on our children," it should be noted that Matthew records no sudden voice booming down from the sky in reply, "So be it!" (27:25)

Responsible Christian theology emphasizes that it was God— not any Jewish prosecution—who was ultimately responsible for the crucifixion, since all mankind was involved in, and affected by, the events swirling around the cross, not just one or another ethnic group. Finally, to be anti-Semitic because of Good Friday would be as ridiculous as hating Italians because Nero once threw Christians to the lions. The only final blunder would be to try and claim that Nero never persecuted Christians, because the records that claim he did must have a hopelessly anti-Italian bias!

8

AT SKULL PLACE

So they took Jesus, and he went out, bearing his own cross, to the place called the place of a skull, which is called in Hebrew Golgotha. There they crucified him, and with him two others, one on either side, and Jesus between them. Pilate also wrote a title and put it on the cross; it read, "Jesus of Nazareth, the King of the Jews."

JOHN 19:17–19

PERHAPS CRUCIFIXION was not *the* most painful death a person could suffer—there are records of human torments that exceeded in duration and intensity what a crucified victim would endure—but it was one of the slower and more brutal forms of execution known to man, and certainly the most public. From the moment the judgment went against him, the condemned victim was *on display:* he had to shoulder his thirty- or forty-pound wooden *patibulum* or crossbeam and carry it in a hideously public parade out to the place of execution, where it would be fastened to one of the upright stakes already standing there. The victim's extremities were bound or nailed to the cross, and he was left to hang, sometimes for several days before he died, as a public example and warning to others to avoid *his* crime, which was plainly stated in the *titulus,* a placard posted above his head.

Crucifixion was invented in the ancient Near East, and one of the earliest accounts of mass execution via the cross was Darius I's crucifixion of 3,000 political enemies in Babylon in 519 B.C. The Romans learned it from their blood enemies the Carthaginians, who regularly used to crucify their admirals for losing sea battles to Rome. Cicero termed it "the cruelest and most hideous punishment" possible, and it was never inflicted on Roman citizens but reserved for slaves, pirates, and those political or religious rebels who had to suffer an exemplary death. Tortured by cramped muscles, unable to swat crawling and buzzing insects, hungry, thirsty, and naked before a taunting crowd, the victims had painfully few ways to retaliate. They might curse back at their tormentors, try spitting on them, or urinate triumphantly in their faces, as in the case of the slaves crucified after the Spartacus revolt.

Some writers have doubted that victims were ever nailed to the cross, claiming that the spikes would have torn through their flesh and failed to support them. But in the summer of 1968, archaeologist V. Tzaferis excavated some stone ossuaries in East Jerusalem dating from the first century A.D. These were chests in which bones of the dead were reburied after the flesh had decomposed following original burial in a cave. One of these ossuaries, inscribed with the name Yohanan Ben Ha'galgol, contained the bones of a man who had obviously been crucified, the first such victim ever discovered. A large, rusty iron spike, seven inches long, had been driven through both heel bones after first penetrating an acacia wood wedge or plaque that held the ankles firmly to the cross. The nail must have encountered a knot on being driven into the cross, for the point of the spike had been bent directly backward. Slivers still clinging to it show that the cross was made of olive wood.

Israeli pathologist Dr. Nicu Haas further examined Yohanan's bones and announced the following conclusions: the victim was between twenty-four and twenty-eight years old, with a triangular face, curved nose, robust chin, and good teeth, but he had a cleft palate on the right side. In addition to the iron spike, evidence of crucifixion included a deep scratch on the right radius bone, showing that a nail had penetrated between the two bones of his lower forearm just above the wrist, which abraded them as the victim writhed in agony.

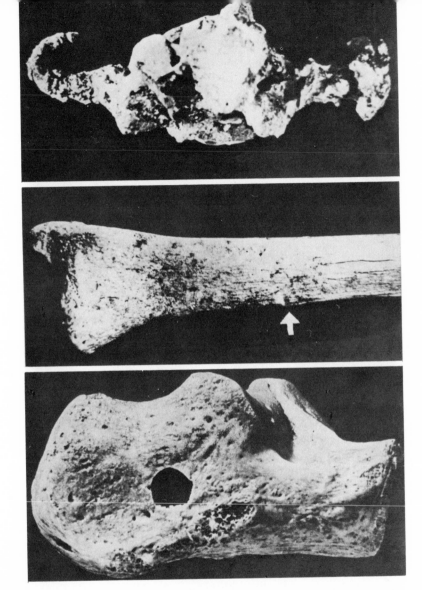

Recently discovered bones of the victim crucified in Jerusalem at the time of Jesus. The upper photograph shows the heel bones as discovered, coated with calcareous crust and pierced by the seven-inch iron spike whose tip encountered a knot and was bent back. In the center is the distal end of the right arm bone, the arrow indicating where a nail scratched the radius. The lower view is of the left heel bone, showing where the spike penetrated from the lateral side.

Yohanan, at any rate, had his lower arms pierced with nails, not his hands, but there were numerous variations of crucifixion. Even the detail of the two criminals having their legs broken at the close of Good Friday to induce death—the *crurifragium*—has an exact parallel here: Yohanan's right tibia and the left tibia and fibula were all broken in their lowest third segment at the same level, indicating a common crushing blow, probably from a mallet or sledge.

What was Yohanan's crime? Something doubtless political, although we shall never know precisely what sent this probable contemporary of Jesus to the cross.

The Via Dolorosa

The route Jesus was forced to take on his final journey to the cross came to be called, long ago, the "Sorrowful Road." A centurion preceded him who was dressed in Roman uniform, even though he was probably a Syrian or Samaritan auxiliary. Four soldiers formed the execution detail itself, but probably all of the 600 in Pilate's Jerusalem cohort were lining the roadsides to control any demonstrations.

Those that did break out were peaceful enough. Evidently a great crowd of people, including numerous women, bewailed and lamented his fate. By now news of Jesus' arrest and condemnation was spreading through Jerusalem, but too late for his followers to try to save him. Turning to them, Jesus said, "Daughters of Jerusalem, do not weep for me, but weep for yourselves and for your children," continuing with his prophecy of the destruction of Jerusalem, which would take place thirty-seven years later.

This is a very important scene that is too often overlooked. How many sermons have been preached on "the fickle mob that could shout *'Hosanna!'* on Palm Sunday and then *'Crucify him!'* on Good Friday." This interpretation, however, would seem faulty. To be sure, some people may have changed their minds about

Jesus, but the shouting multitude in front of Pilate's tribunal consisted primarily of the priest-controlled Temple staff—their police alone numbered 10,000—whereas some of the Palm Sunday people were just now getting the news about Jesus' conviction and rushing to the roadside in tears, as in this scene.

By now it was high noon. Two other condemned men were also grunting under their crossbeams on the way out to Golgotha, a pair of felons about whom nothing is known. Jesus' scourging must have been more brutal or more recent than theirs, because he stumbled and collapsed under his crossbeam, and the troops had to impress a bystander, Simon from Cyrene in North Africa, into carrying the beam for him. Some have thought Simon a black, others a Jew attending the Passover in Jerusalem, but the experience of carrying the cross may have converted him. Mark says that he was "the father of Alexander and Rufus," who were obviously known to Christian readers of his Gospel (15:21), and Rufus' name crops up again at the close of Paul's letter to Rome (16:13).

When they reached Golgotha, the execution detail offered the condemned men a drink of wine mixed with myrrh as a narcotic. Jesus tasted but would not swallow it. Perhaps he alone remembered that now, at the end of his life, came several incredible reminders of its beginning: myrrh had been given him by the Magi at the Nativity, and they had come to this very city asking for a newborn "King of the Jews." Astonishingly, this was precisely the charge that was now being nailed onto the central vertical post that would form his cross.

Where Was Golgotha?

Just as two different sites have been suggested for Jesus' trial before Pilate, so two locations are offered for Skull Place, yet only one of these has any historical support. Many current tourists prefer the other—the so-called "Gordon's Calvary"—since there is a somewhat skull-shaped hillock overlooking the Damascus Gate of Jerusalem, which British General Charles "Chinese"

The Church of the Holy Sepulcher in Jerusalem, built over the traditional sites of Golgotha (approximately under the small cupola in the foreground) and the tomb of Joseph of Arimathea in which Jesus was buried (under the largest dome).

Gordon assumed was the crucifixion site in 1883, just two years before he was killed at Khartoum. But, attractive as the location is, Gordon's Calvary and the nearby "Garden Tomb" in which Jesus was presumably buried have no ancient historical traditions to authenticate them.

The traditional site, the Church of the Holy Sepulcher, does. As in the case of the Nativity at Bethlehem, the story goes back to the Roman emperor Hadrian (117–138 A.D.), who tried to Romanize Jerusalem by obliterating its sacred sites. Over the precincts of Golgotha and the sepulcher in which Jesus was buried he erected a temple to Venus, patroness of Rome, but in trying thereby to erase the locations he merely preserved their identity.

In 325 A.D., when Bishop Macarius of Jerusalem was attending the first ecumenical council at Nicea, he persuaded Constantine the Great, first Christian emperor of Rome, to assist him in restoring the sacred sites. In the following year, the emperor's mother Helena made a pilgrimage to Jersalem and directly contributed to the work, which finally saw several structures erected where the Church of the Holy Sepulcher now stands. Although the complex of buildings around Golgotha has been destroyed and rebuilt several times, and the present structure gathering them all under one roof dates back only to Crusader times, the sites of Calvary and the tomb are the same as those uncovered seventeen centuries ago.

The present Church of the Holy Sepulcher, however, is usually disappointing to the modern visitor because almost nothing seems right about it. It stands squarely inside the present Old City of Jerusalem, when the crucifixion certainly took place outside. Moreover, the Church would seem to link Calvary and the sepulcher much too closely together, barely fifty yards, and the aesthetic disappointment inside the structure is almost suffocating. And yet all these objections are easily explainable.

It must be remembered that Jerusalem has certainly expanded since Jesus' day to include inside it what used to be the execution hillock standing originally outside the Ephraim gate in the north-western wall. Excavations by Kathleen Kenyon in 1967 have un-covered an ancient quarry south of the Church of the Holy Sepul-cher, further indicating that this general sector stood beyond the walls of Jerusalem in early New Testament times, since ancients went outside of their closely packed towns to quarry stone. And other tombs discovered just west of the Holy Sepulcher prove that this site lay outside Jerusalem at one time, since burials were never permitted within the walls.

But could the sepulcher have been located only a scant 150 feet northwest of Golgotha? Would the wealthy Joseph of Arimathea have had his new tomb, in which Jesus was buried, hewn so close to an area of public execution? Astonishingly, yes. Execution and burial grounds lay very close to each other in ancient towns, and this location near one of Jerusalem's principal gates would have been prestigious. According to the Fourth Gospel, "Now *in* the place where he was crucified there was a garden, and in the garden a new tomb where no one had ever been laid. . . . the tomb was *close at hand*" (19:41–42).

Constantine's engineers constructed a great marble basilica around and to the north of the Golgotha hillock, and then built a separate monument over the Easter tomb. Originally, Joseph's sepulcher was a simple excavation in living rock, but the Roman engineers cut the surrounding matrix away from the tomb and erected a great domed *tholos* or colonnade around it. Finally, the Crusaders linked Golgotha, the basilica, and the resurrection *tholos* under one roof, which is the present Church of the Holy Sepulcher.

Western visitors are usually disappointed by the potpourri of garish votive lanterns and chapels that cluster about the sacred sites. After entering from the south portal of the Church, the traditional site of Calvary is reached by climbing up some natural rock to a sanctuary sixteen feet above the floor of the basilica, the rise of Golgotha. At the end of the sanctuary stands the Altar of the Cross, constructed over outcroppings of living rock that still

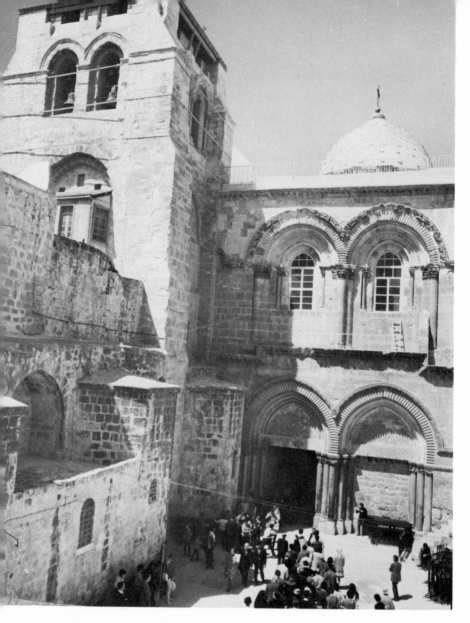

The entrance and southern façade of the Church of the Holy Sepulcher in Jerusalem. A Good Friday procession is about to enter the basilica, whose right doorway has been walled up since the time of Saladin.

show a fissure caused by the earthquake attending Jesus' death, according to tradition. Under the altar is a silver disk with an opening in the center, presumably marking the spot where Jesus' cross was erected. On each side of the altar are black marble disks where the crosses of the two robbers were supposedly fixed, but such locational precision, of course, is extremely doubtful.

Fifty yards to the northwest under an ancient rotunda stands the sepulcher. The excessively ornate edicule erected over the tomb and the artificial setting in general seem a poor contrast to the usual vivid impressions of the first Easter. But during Holy Week each year, the entire basilica quivers with worshipers who recapitulate Jesus' final journey, death, and resurrection in an atmosphere of burning wax and incense, while the vast reaches of the structure reecho the chanting and singing of many thousands of pilgrims. The most spectacular moment is the lighting of the Holy Fire on Easter eve, when the Greek Orthodox patriarch hands a burning candle out from the sepulcher into the basilica, where worshipers light their own tapers from his in expanding jubilation.

The Seven Last Statements

Back in time to the first Good Friday, Jesus had just refused the narcotic wine and now the execution detail stripped off his clothes. They divided his garments into four shares, one for each auxiliary, but they had to cast lots for his cloak since it was seamless. Perhaps it was the white robe Herod Antipas had awarded the mock king. At any rate, they shook knucklebone dice for it, and we have no idea who won.

Jesus' hands were nailed to the crossbeam, which was then lowered onto a vertical stake at Golgotha, and his feet were spiked onto it. He was probably made to straddle a wedge placed between his legs, as in other crucifixions, which would have borne his weight sufficiently so that the nailed hands would not, in fact, have torn apart.

Jesus maintained this agonizing position "from the sixth to the ninth hour," that is, from noon till about 3 P.M. Sneers from the claque gathered around the crosses focused on a rather obvious theme: the wonder-worker who supposedly saved others could not even save his own skin. The soldiers mocked him in similar vein, "If you *are* the King of the Jews, save yourself!"

The New Testament records seven final statements that Jesus made from the cross. There may well have been more, but these are the only ones reported. Not one of them was vindictive, yet the first did address itself to the taunts from below, "Father, forgive them; for they know not what they do."

One of the felons crucified next to Jesus harped on the same, rather unimaginative theme as the voices below, "Are you not the Christ? Save yourself—*and us!*" But his misery was seizing on anything—anything—to make him forget the present horror, even for a moment.

What happed next is familiar, but never ceases to amaze. The comrade of the felon proceeds to tell him off for this imperti-nence, admits their common guilt and Jesus' innocence, and then turns to the center cross with the plea, "Jesus, remember me when you come in your kingly power."

Jesus replies, "Truly I say to you, today you will be with me in Paradise."

Of all the disciples, John alone had the courage to show up at Calvary, and he was standing near the foot of the cross with the three prime Marys in Jesus' life: his mother, whose heart must have been slowly breaking; his Aunt Mary, wife of Clopas; and Mary Magdalene. From the cross itself he made final provision for his mother in the famous statement, "Woman, behold your son." And then to John, "Behold your mother." From then on John did indeed treat Mary as a mother, for earliest Christian traditions link Mary and John from Jerusalem to far-off Ephesus.

By now the sky had darkened ominously, as if the eastern Mediterranean were shadowed by a solar eclipse. Because of the full moon, however, it could not possibly have been an eclipse.

Glowering April skies are not unknown in Palestine, and sometimes dark siroccos or windstorms blow in from the desert, plunging the countryside into an uncanny darkness. Did the meteorological mood affect even Jesus? For he cried out, in the daily Aramaic spoken in Palestine, the opening words of Psalm 22: *"Eli, Eli lama sabbachthani?* My God, my God, why hast thou forsaken me?"

Shortly afterward he uttered his fifth comment from the cross, the only slight complaint that entire Friday, "I am thirsty." The soldiers stuck a sponge on a javelin, dipped it in a bowl of their common military *posca*—a sour but thirst-quenching combination of vinegar and water—and held it up to Jesus' lips. After sucking a little of it, Jesus announced the consummation of his mission,

Under the Chapel of Calvary in the Church of the Holy Sepulcher, the presumed living rock of Golgotha can still be seen through special openings. This view shows a cleft in the rock caused by the earthquake attending Jesus' death, according to tradition.

"It is finished." And then, in an even louder voice, his last words, "Father, into thy hands I commit my spirit." One last breath, and he died.

The spectacular events surrounding his death—the earthquake, the torn veil of the Temple, the centurion's comment—do not detract from the solemnity of the moment: Jesus of Nazareth, who for three incredible years had transformed the multitudes, was dead.

Was he surely dead? So that the three victims would not have to hang on their crosses after sundown and into the Passover sabbath, the priests requested that the *crurifragium* be inflicted. The execution detail broke the legs of the two felons, inducing immediate death. But when they approached the center cross, they saw that Jesus had already died. Still, as an executioner's gesture and to make assurance doubly sure, one of the men shoved a spear into Jesus' side. Blood and water flowed out of the wound, probably pericardial fluid or extravasated blood that had separated into its constituent red cells and plasma, possibly indicating a heart rupture. Or whatever else a pathologist might judge, Jesus was dead indeed.

The Burial

It was Joseph of Arimathea who asked Pilate's permission to remove the body of Jesus from the cross and bury it. Joseph was a wealthy member of the Sanhedrin who had not voted to condemn Jesus and was doubtless a disciple in secret. Although Romans had no requirement that a victim's body be removed from the cross—indeed, they often left corpses hanging indefinitely until picked clean by vultures—Jewish law was far more humane, requiring burial of a criminal on the same day as his execution (Deut. 21:23). Bowing to local custom in the matter, Pilate readily allowed Joseph to inter the body of Jesus, wondering only that he had died so soon.

Typical Jewish sepulchers of the time—and Joseph's must have

The altar of the Crucifixion within the Calvary Chapel in the Church of the Holy Sepulcher. Jesus' central cross presumably stood at the altar area. To the left, a Greek Orthodox monk supervises the sanctuary.

been one of these—had two chambers hollowed out of rock, the first serving as a vestibule or entranceway into the tomb proper, which was a small squarish room with a shelf built into the far wall where the corpse was laid. Outside, the doorway into the vestibule was closed by a very heavy circular stone that rolled down a slightly inclined runway or channel until it shut the sepulcher.

Nicodemus, another Sanhedrist who was a disciple in secret, helped his colleague Joseph in the burial process. He brought a great bundle of spices—myrrh and aloes—and placed these between the folds of the eight-foot linen shroud that he and Joseph wound around the body of Jesus, the standard Jewish practice. There was also a separate, smaller piece of gravecloth in which they wrapped Jesus' head and then placed it on a pillow of stones, as was customary. Some of the loyal women from Galilee watched the pair at work, intending to improve the necessarily hasty job as soon as the Sabbath was past. Finally Joseph kicked away the wedge holding the door stone in its upper channel, and the great circle of rock grumbled down its track, shutting the sepulcher.

The silver disk under the altar of the Crucifixion in the Church of the Holy Sepulcher marks the traditional spot where Jesus' cross stood at Golgotha.

Only the Passover Seder that evening prevented the chief priests and Pharisees from asking Pilate any earlier, but the next morning they appeared at his palace with the following request, "Sir, we remember how that imposter said, while he was still alive, 'After three days I will rise again.' Therefore order the sepulcher to be made secure until the third day, lest his disciples go and steal him away, and tell the people, 'He has risen from the dead,' and the last fraud will be worse than the first."

Amazed at a fanaticism that could hound a man not only to his grave, but beyond it, Pilate replied, "You have a guard of soldiers; go, make it as secure as you can" (Mt. 27:63 ff.).

Summoning a detachment of Temple police, they went to Joseph's tomb and secured the area, sealing the stone and stationing a guard. The seal was nothing more than a cord strung across the rock and fastened at each end with clay. Like any seal, its purpose was not to cement the rock but to indicate any tampering with it.

9

EASTER DAWN

And when the Sabbath was past, Mary Magdalene, and Mary the mother of James, and Salome, bought spices, so that they might go and anoint him. And very early on the first day of the week they went to the tomb when the sun had risen. And they were saying to one another, "Who will roll away the stone for us from the door of the tomb?" And looking up, they saw that the stone was rolled back; for it was very large.

MARK 16:1–4

WHAT *DID* HAPPEN AT DAWN on Sunday morning? If it were somehow possible to get an authentic replay of an event from the past, probably more people would opt for the first Easter than any other episode in history. Or, if Jesus had lived in the twentieth century instead, his grave would probably have been guarded in a different fashion: scientists would have installed sensory devices both inside and outside the sepulcher; medical experts would have been scanning computers recording any of Jesus' life signs—or lack of them; theologians and philosophers would have recorded their impressions on tape; while photographers would have been ready to focus anything visible on film of every kind. Or *would* any of this have happened? Possibly the hints Jesus dropped about "rising on the third day" would have gone just as unheeded today as then.

Because scientific and scholarly measurement of the events on Sunday morning did not take place, but the resurrection itself did —so the earliest narratives claim—the Easter phenomenon has been vigorously denied, doubted, disregarded, believed, or enthusiastically proclaimed ever since. The central event of history, then, is also its most controversial.

The resurrection accounts in the New Testament—magnificent, joyful, triumphant narratives that they are—do present some startling variations on a common theme. One *or* two *or* three *or* more women approach the sepulcher at Easter dawn, according to John, Matthew, Mark, and Luke respectively. One angel greets them with the resurrection announcement in Matthew and Mark, while two do in Luke and John. Luke confines the resurrection appearances to the Jerusalem area, but the other three involve Galilee as well, and there are other problems of sequence that have bedeviled conservative scholars and cheered the critics.

First of all, it is no service either to Christianity or to honesty to gloss over these discrepancies, or, as is incredibly done in some circles, to deny that they exist. A seriatim reading of the last chapter in each of the Gospels will identify them plainly enough, and burying one's head in the sands of faith to hide from their existence is merely the posture of an ostrich.

On the other hand, some critical scholars are equally mistaken in seeking to use these inconsistencies as some kind of proof that the resurrection did not take place, for this is an illogical use of evidence. The earliest sources telling of the great fire of Rome, for example, offer far more serious conflicts on who or what started the blaze and how far it spread, some claiming that the whole city was scorched while others insist that only three sectors were reduced to ash. Yet the fire itself is historical: it actually happened.

Now, if such variations in the New Testament showed up *only* in the resurrection accounts, then the problem would be far more serious than it is. But all four Gospels contain similar variations in relating previous episodes in the life of Jesus, so the accounts of the first Easter are simply more of the same.

This leads to a point that has not been sufficiently stressed: actually, the variations in the resurrection narratives *tend to sup-*

The traditional site of Calvary is indicated by the small hillock at left center in this model of ancient Jerusalem designed by Avi-Yonah although it lay somewhat farther away from the wall than the angle of this photograph would suggest. In the foreground stands the tomb of the Hasmonean John Hyrcanus, who ruled Palestine from 135 to 104 B.C., while the four towers of the Fortress Antonia command the background. Here the 600 auxiliaries in Pilate's Jerusalem cohort were barracked, and here Peter (Acts 12) and Paul (Acts 23) were taken into custody.

port, rather than undermine, their authenticity. They demonstrate that there were several independent traditions stemming from some event which must indeed have happened to give rise to them. And the fact that they were not harmonized by some ancient church editor shows that there was no agreed upon—and therefore partially fabricated—version.

Even eyewitnesses can report the same event differently. In a common classroom demonstration of this fact, a professor stages some episode—perhaps a crime being perpetrated—and then, on the next day, he asks his students to record their impressions. The variations in their reports are stunning. Certainly the Easter witnesses, in reporting something as incredibly exciting as what they claimed to see, would tell their stories in similar, yet different ways.

The Women

Women play a more enviable role than men in the events of Holy Week. In contrast to the misunderstandings, betrayals, denials, and flight of the male followers of Jesus, it was women who anointed Jesus at Bethany, who punctured Peter's pretenses in the courtyard of Caiaphas, who warned Pilate to release Jesus because he was innocent, who commiserated his fate on the way to Golgotha, and who stood loyally under the cross until the end.

And it was women who were the first witnesses to the events of Easter morning. Just before dawn that Sunday, Mary Magdalene, Mary (mother of James), Salome, and Joanna brought aromatic oils to anoint the body of Jesus. The Sabbath had prevented their doing this earlier, and they wished to improve on the necessarily hasty burial given Jesus by Joseph of Arimathea and Nicodemus. All of these women were Galilean followers of Jesus who had supported his ministry in the north country, also financially, and had now accompanied him to Jerusalem. Salome was probably the mother of the disciples James and John, while

Joanna had important political connections: she was the wife of Herod Antipas' chief steward, Chuza.

But the story focuses primarily on Mary Magdalene, the only woman mentioned in all four Easter gospels. She came from the coastal town of Magdala at the westernmost bulge of the Sea of Galilee, a place so notorious that it besmirched also Mary's reputation, for tradition has made of her an ex-prostitute. However, there is no real evidence that Mary had actually been plying the world's oldest profession, and after Jesus cured her unidentified but serious illness, she became one of his most devoted followers. The Fourth Gospel offers her most luminous portrait: the woman weeping at the empty tomb, talking with the risen Jesus whom, in her blurred vision, she thought a gardener, and finally radiantly recognizing him.

But before this or any of the other appearances, the women approaching Joseph's tomb had a substantial problem on their hands: "Who will roll away the stone for us from the door of the tomb?" The circle of rock shutting off the entrance was "very large" according to Matthew and Mark, while two ancient Gospel manuscripts add that it was a stone "which twenty men could scarcely roll." Certainly this is an exaggerated embellishment, though it is true that it would require more strength to move such a gravestone up to an open position than to close it, due to its sloping channel.

Evidently the women were also unaware that the stone had been sealed, and that the whole area was under military guard. Had nothing else happened that Sunday morning, the soldiers would simply have refused them admission to the sepulcher and the women would have returned, spices heavy in hand. Then we would probably never even have heard of one Jesus of Nazareth, and Easter would be nothing more than a pagan spring fertility festival named for Eostre or Ostara, the reputed Anglo-Saxon goddess of the dawn.

But the Gospels claim that a momentous phenomenon occurred, and the rest of this chapter is a reconstruction of the New Testament accounts. The earth shook, the gravestone was dis- lodged and rolled open, the guards trembled and "became like dead men," and an angel announced to the understandably ter- rified women, "Do not be afraid; for I know that you seek Jesus who was crucified. He is not here; for he has risen, as he said. Come, see the place where he lay. Then go quickly and tell his disciples that he has risen from the dead" (Mt. 28:5–7).

With the most contrary emotions coursing through them to test their sanity, the women fled from the tomb in both fear and joy to tell the disciples. Matthew records Jesus himself intercept- ing them in his first resurrection appearance with the salutation, "Hail!" Now surer of the event, they took hold of his feet and worshiped him in an ecstasy of gladness. "Do not be afraid," Jesus said. "Go and tell my brothers to go to Galilee, and there they will see me."

The Men

The women hurried off to the disciples with their incredible tidings, but the Eleven greeted their reports with unanimous disbelief. "Idle tales!" "Hysterical women!" or "The demons have returned to Mary Magdalene" may have been the more charitable comments.

Indeed, the fact that *women* served as the first witnesses to the resurrection was later something of an embarrassment for the disciples. Not that they were jealous of them for getting the first glimpse, as it were, but women did not have the right to bear witness in Jewish courts—their testimony, in that day, was deemed unreliable—so the initial reaction of the Eleven was un- derstandably one of suspicion and disbelief. Again, if the resur- rection accounts had been manufactured out of whole cloth, women would *never* have been included in the story, at least, not as first witnesses.

Perhaps for this reason there may have been a change of plans

Exterior façade of the edicule constructed over the presumed sepulcher in which Jesus was buried, now under the rotunda of the Church of the Holy Sepulcher.

at least implied in the Gospels: Jesus, Luke and John report, appeared to the disciples in Jerusalem even before their planned reunion in Galilee, or there might have been no reunion at all with the disciples refusing to make the trip just on the word of the women.

Two of the men, however, had reason to give some credence to the women's reports. Peter and John, after hearing Mary Magdalene tell of the missing body, raced to the tomb—John got there first—and they both went inside the sepulcher. There they saw the linen gravecloths in two parts: the main linen bands lying flat, pressed down by the eighty-pound weight of the spices, and the separate napkin, which had covered Jesus' head, still in a bunched-up, rolled condition at the end of the stone slab on which his body had lain, retaining its shape because of its smaller size. According to this literal interpretation of the Greek in which John was written, it seemed as if the body simply vanished from its grave wrappings, leaving them exactly in place except for gravity flattening the main shroud.

Peter and John, at any rate, knew for a fact that Jesus' body was missing, even if they did not yet believe in its revivification. Their doubt, however, lasted no longer than twelve hours, because on Easter evening came the first general appearance of Jesus to his disciples. In despair over the evident failure of Jesus' mission, and in fear that the priestly aristocracy in Jerusalem might persecute them too, ten of the Eleven were huddled behind locked doors when suddenly Jesus appeared to them and said, "Peace be with you." Evidently he had materialized through the walls, and the disciples—in their usual posture in such instances—were merely terrified. Only spirits behaved in that fashion.

But this was only the same "ghost" who had once frightened them while walking on the Sea of Galilee. "Why are you troubled?" Jesus asked. Then, showing them his pierced extremities, he said, "Look at my hands and my feet, that it is I myself. Touch me, and see, for a spirit does not have flesh and bones as you see that I have."

The mood among the disciples was shifting instantaneously from disbelief to radiant joy. As a kind of final visual aid, Jesus even asked them, "Do you have anything here to eat?" They gave him a piece of broiled fish, a dish appropriate enough for a partial crew of ex-fishermen. Jesus took the fish and ate it, hardly the gesture expected of a specter. None of the Gospels was fully able to convey the incredible happiness at the reunion between the Teacher and his disciples.

Then it was time for one of Jesus' final discourses with them, in which he directly keyed his mission to Old Testament prophecy, adding, "Thus it is written, that the Christ should suffer and on the third day rise from the dead, and that repentance and forgiveness of sins should be preached in his name to all nations, beginning from Jerusalem. You are witnesses of these things" (Lk. 24:46 ff.).

Indeed, in view of his own prediction that he would rise on the third day—so specific that the Temple authorities tried to forestall a grave robbery—and against the background of his already demonstrated success in dealing with death, perhaps the event at Easter dawn should not have been *that* surprising to the Eleven.

One of the disciples, however, was missing from this glad reunion, Thomas the Twin. The sources do not tell us what had detained him. Conceivably, Thomas was out, trying to shape a new life for himself after three years he may have thought wasted in the wrong cause. Then, when his colleagues broke the happy news to him, "We have seen the Lord!" Thomas simply balked. Evidently they also mentioned Jesus' marks of identification, the crucifixion scars, for Thomas challenged that point directly, "Unless *I* see in his hands the print of the nails, and place *my* finger in the mark of the nails, and place *my* hand in his side, I will not believe."

For this remark, future ages would call Thomas a fool, a dullard, a doubter, or, more charitably, a skeptic. Germans in the Middle Ages used the ass as the sign of this apostle in ridiculing his disbelief, but the modern era tends instead to applaud Thomas' demand for empirical proof. His was a scientific challenge, a demand for direct and objective, not hearsay, evidence that would reach his five senses. The tales of excited women were not enough. The supposed apparition deluding his colleagues was not enough. But his personally touching the scars would indeed be enough—if that were possible.

A week later, the disciples were gathered at the same place, only this time Thomas was with them. Again Jesus appeared to them with the Hebrew greeting, *"Shalom!"*—"Peace be with

Interior of the edicule in the Church of the Holy Sepulcher, the marble slab marking the traditional place where Jesus lay. Nothing, however, remains of the original tomb but the rock foundation, since the caliph Al Hakem brutally demolished the Church of the Holy Sepulcher in 1009 A. D., and a successor razed the tomb to the ground.

you!" Then he walked purposefully over to Thomas and met him on his own terms, "Put your finger here, and see my hands; and put out your hand, and place it in my side; do not be faithless, but believing."

Overcome, Thomas could only manage an exultant, "My Lord and my God!"

"Have you believed because you have seen me?" Jesus chided him, gently. "Blessed are those who have not seen and yet believe" (Jn. 20:26 ff.).

Other Appearances

That comment focused largely on the future. For the present, most of those who believed had also, like Thomas, seen the risen Jesus, for he made other climactic appearances—Luke calls them "many proofs" (Acts 1:3)—over the next forty days. Sometimes he came in a very unobtrusive and casual manner, as he already had on the afternoon of Easter Sunday, when he appeared to two of his followers on the road to Emmaus. Cleopas and his unnamed friend, both probably members of the larger group of seventy of Jesus' disciples (Lk. 10:1), were walking the seven-mile trip from the Holy City when Jesus joined them as a fellow traveler. They failed to recognize him until they had supper together in Emmaus, after which they raced back to Jerusalem and told the disciples.

There were specialized appearances to individual followers for a specific purpose: to Simon Peter, apparently as a reconfirmation in apostleship after his denial, as well as to his brother James, the future bishop of Jerusalem.

There were additional appearances to the disciples, including two unforgettable scenes among their familiar haunts up in the north country. In one, a poignant recapitulation of their first meeting with the Teacher, the disciples were again fishing on the Sea of Galilee when they followed piscatorial directives from the Man on shore and brought him 153 fish for their breakfast. In another, on a mountain in Galilee, Jesus appeared not only to the Eleven but also to at least five hundred in a broader circle of his followers. And at the final parting on the Mount of Olives, the disciples witnessed Jesus' ascension, i.e., his withdrawal into another dimension.

In one of the earliest records of the Easter event, written before any of the gospels, Paul would pen these words to readers in the city of Corinth:

For I delivered to you as of first importance what I also received, that Christ died for our sins in accordance with the scriptures, that he was buried, that he was raised on the third day in accordance with the scriptures, and that he appeared to Cephas [Peter], then to the twelve. Then he appeared to more than five hundred brethren at one time, most of whom are still alive, though some have fallen asleep. Then he appeared to James, then to all the apostles. Last of all, as to one untimely born, he appeared also to me" (1 Cor. 15:3–8).

The last, of course, referred to the episode on the Damascus road. Paul wrote this statement only a score of years after the first Easter.

10

DOUBTS AND CRITICISM

If Christ has not been raised, then our preaching is in vain and your faith is in vain. . . . If for this life only we have hoped in Christ, we are of all men most to be pitied.

1 CORINTHIANS 15:14,19

PAUL'S BELIEF IN THE RESURRECTION, shared by early Christianity, was absolute and categorical. Anything less than Jesus' actual, physical, historical triumph over death would have vitiated the cause to which he had staked his life, and rendered Christians in general a pitiable lot.

Nevertheless, the apostle's exuberant faith has not been universally shared since the first Easter, and a literal resurrection of Jesus' body has been denied not only by non-Christians but generally also by liberal theology. The opposition stems from this basic argument: a physical resurrection, like the other so-called miracles in the Bible, could never have happened, since natural laws simply cannot be suspended. The dead are not raisable today; nor were they then.

Since, however, *something* must have taken place on Easter morning to have ignited that spiritual explosion called Christianity, critics have advanced the following hypotheses to explain some of the phenomena noted at the first Easter.

The stolen body theory. This is the oldest and simplest explanation for an empty tomb. Jesus' body was removed by the disciples either in order to protect it from possible desecration or to hatch the myth of a risen Christ. Or Joseph of Arimathea, who had first hastily buried Jesus in a cave near the execution site, later gave the body permanent, secret burial in his own tomb. Conversely, he may have had second thoughts about his charitable action in burying a criminal and therefore removed the body so it would not contaminate his tomb. Or Pontius Pilate may have ordered its secret removal to forestall any cult of martyrdom at the grave site. At any rate, when the women came to the original tomb at Sunday dawn, they would have found it empty.

The wrong-tomb theory. Because of Jesus' hasty burial and the fact that they came in dim morning light, the women were not sure exactly which of the many rock-hewn tombs in the area was Joseph's. When they examined the wrong one, which was empty, they were startled by a gardener or grave worker (whom they thought an angel) who guessed their mission and tried to correct their mistake. "He is not here," the gardener advised, and then pointed to the correct sepulcher, "See the place where he lay." But the women panicked, fled, and later announced an empty tomb.

The "lettuce" theory is an alternate of the above. The gardener was so piqued at curiosity-seekers trampling over lettuce seedlings he had planted in the garden around Joseph's tomb that he removed the body of Jesus and reinterred it elsewhere. But still visitors came to the now-empty sepulcher and proclaimed the resurrection. Crude as this hypothesis sounds, it was, in fact, one of the early non-Christian explanations for the resurrection, and the second-century church father Tertullian himself records it.

The swoon theory. Jesus never really died. He only appeared to die, but, perhaps due to the effect of some deep narcotic administered to him on the cross, he lingered on in a state of suspended animation. After his burial, the cool of the tomb and the healing effect of the spices wrapped around his body revived him. Exchanging his grave clothes for those of a gardener, he somehow managed to crawl out of the sepulcher and then encountered Mary Magdalene. After her glad recognition, he made his way to Joseph or the disciples, who nursed him back to health and presented him as the risen Lord. Forty days later, his wounds got the better of him, but just before he expired, he assembled the disciples on a mountain and parted from them by walking into a cloud. Though he was crawling off to die, the Eleven believed he had ascended into heaven. Various forms of this theory have been suggested ever since the pagan philosopher Celsus in the second century A.D. first proposed it.

The psychological or hallucination theory. The various visions or appearances of Jesus were merely the psychic effects of profound wish fulfillment. When one of the women claimed to see the resurrected Jesus, the experience became contagious and soon others "saw" him, too, including finally the disciples also. Jesus' prophecies of his triumph over death had primed his followers to expect exactly that, and so the whole myth began with "the visions of a half-frantic woman," according to Celsus.

Others, such as the nineteenth-century German scholar David Strauss, have suggested that one of the disciples, perhaps Peter, sustained the original hallucination. According to this scenario, the Eleven fled to Galilee after the crucifixion, where they finally calmed down and reflected on Jesus. The impulsive Peter in particular was meditating on his dead master when suddenly he had a sensation or vision of Jesus' surviving presence. Peter himself could not know that this was just a fantasy of his own imagination because, like his contemporaries who believed in ghosts and spirits, he would have been unable to distinguish between a real incursion from another dimension and a subjective hallucination. Peter's enthusiasm quickly became contagious, and when confused and exaggerated reports were received from the women in Jerusalem, the disciples, clutching at every resurrection rumor, returned joyously to the Holy City and proclaimed the new faith. Unconsciously, they began pushing back the date of Peter's vision until it was fixed at the third day after the crucifixion, influenced by such prophecies as Hosea 6:2: "On the third day he will raise us up. . . ." They did all this not as frauds or liars, but in good faith.

The Garden Tomb in northern Jerusalem, showing the channel in which the circular doorstone—now missing—moved. This first- or second-century Jewish sepulcher is partially walled in.

The twin brother theory. Jesus had an exact twin brother, who substituted for him on occasion but generally stayed out of sight. When Jesus truly died on Friday, the twin emerged triumphantly from seclusion on Sunday and people beheld the risen Lord.

Other theories, such as the rapid-decay hypothesis, are not worth the listing. In Palestine's hot climate, supposedly, the process of organic putrefaction was accelerated, and the sepulcher was not visited until the body had fully decayed. But in only three days, this would have been manifestly impossible.

Certainly these various theories stand as tributes to human ingenuity. And they have surely stood the test of time: although all of them are still in current use, nearly all were advanced in one form or another many centuries ago. The different explanations also have this in common: they all require at least as much faith to believe in their validity as in the resurrection itself. For the overpowering weight of all the sources, all circumstantial evidence from the first Easter, and logic itself stands against them.

A Critique of Criticism

The stolen body theory founders on two insurmountable obstacles: the problem of motive and the problem of execution. To plan a tricky grave robbery of a closely guarded tomb would have required an incredibly strong incentive by a daring and extremely skillful group of men. But who had this incentive? Who had the motive and then the courage necessary to bring it off? Certainly not the dispirited disciples, huddling and hiding in their despair over Jesus' evident failure and in fear of the Temple authorities —hardly a pack of calculating schemers enthusiastically planning to dupe their countrymen. Certainly not their discredited leader, Peter, who, unable to stand by Jesus in life, could not possibly have had the audacity to snatch his body in death. Certainly not Joseph of Arimathea or Nicodemus, who were probably already suspected by their Sanhedral colleagues for their attention to Jesus' body. If, as is sometimes argued, they were merely showing

Interior of the Garden Tomb, showing a broken stone slab on which the body of the deceased was placed.

charity to a criminal which they later regretted, why did they not bury and then reinter all three victims that Friday? And certainly Pontius Pilate would have been the last to disturb the body: after permitting the sepulcher to be sealed and guarded, he was glad to have done with the sorry business.

But even if the disciples did have the overpowering motive and the incredible courage to steal a body and then—with total cynicism—to announce a resurrection, how could they hope to achieve it? The grave area was crawling with guards specifically instructed to forestall any such attempt. Certainly there were not so many as "thirty Romans and a thousand Jews," as the Slavonic version of Josephus has it, but it would have been ridiculous to go to the trouble of sealing the sepulcher and setting a watch if it were not more than adequate to handle any nocturnal theft attempt or daytime riot. Later on, Peter would be guarded by four squads of four men each when imprisoned by Herod Agrippa (Acts 12), so sixteen would be a minimum number expected *outside* a prison. Guards in ancient times always slept in shifts, so it would have been virtually impossible for a raiding party to have stepped over all their sleeping faces, as is sometimes claimed. The commotion caused by breaking the seal, rolling the stone open, entering the tomb, and lifting out the body was bound to awaken the guards even if they had all been sleeping.

Admittedly, there was indeed a period of time when the sepulcher was unguarded: the approximately twelve or thirteen hours between the burial of Jesus on Friday evening and the priests' request for a guard from Pilate early Saturday morning. A raiding party *could* have removed the body Friday night while everyone was sleeping off wine from the Passover Seder. Although the New Testament does not record whether or not the guard first rolled back the stone on Saturday morning to make sure the body of Jesus was still inside before sealing it, the most primitive logic would have dictated that they do just that. They would hardly have sealed and guarded an empty tomb. That they did in fact open the grave can easily be concluded from the reaction of the priests when the shaken guards reported the missing body to them: "Tell the people," they were instructed, "that his disciples came by night, and stole him away while you were asleep." Obviously they would have had a *much* better excuse had they found the tomb empty already on Saturday morning, which would not have compromised the soldiers.

The wrong-tomb theory is interesting enough, but Matthew tells of Mary Magdalene and "the other Mary" directly observing the burial of Jesus on Friday evening, when they had specifically gauged the size of the stone, so it seems extremely unlikely that they would have erred. If they had, Joseph of Arimathea or the guards assigned to the sepulcher would certainly have corrected them in the ensuing furore.

The "lettuce" theory introduces a note of humor and nothing more, for the versatile gardener (who evidently transplanted bodies as well as lettuce) would have had some answering to do to the owner of the sepulcher, to say nothing of his having been prevented by the guards in the first place.

The swoon theory is very ingenious, but it rides roughshod over all evidence from the sources—so much so that there was no hint of this theory by any of the early opponents of Christianity. True, there is a recorded instance of a victim being taken down from a cross and surviving. The Jewish historian Josephus, who had gone over to the Roman side in the rebellion of 66 A.D., discovered three of his friends being crucified. He asked the Roman general Titus to reprieve them, and they were immediately removed from their crosses. Still, two of the three died anyway, even though they had apparently been crucified only a short time. In Jesus' case, however, there were the additional complications of scourging and exhaustion, to say nothing of the great spear thrust that pierced his rib cage and probably ruptured his pericardium. Romans were grimly efficient about crucifixions: victims did *not* escape with their lives.

And even if Jesus were history's great exception in this instance, how could a crawling, wounded near-cadaver inspire in his followers the founding of a faith based on his resurrection? Even David Strauss, the critic who propounded the hallucination theory, wrote:

It is impossible that a being who had stolen half-dead out of the sepulcher, who crept about weak and ill, wanting medical treatment, who required bandaging, strengthening, and indulgence, and who still at last yielded to his sufferings, could have given the disciples the impression that he was a conqueror over death and the grave, the Prince of Life: an impression which lay at the bottom of their future ministry.

The psychological or hallucination theory would be attractive if only one person had claimed to see a vision of the risen Christ, perhaps Mary Magdalene, who formerly may have had psychic problems anyway. But the disciples were a hardheaded and hardly hallucinable group, especially Thomas. And—if the sources have any validity—there would have to have been collective hallucinations for different groups of up to five hundred in size, all of them seeing the same thing—a virtual impossibility in the case of a phenomenon that is usually extremely individualistic. Many different people will *not* see the same thing at different places in any general hallucination, mirage, daydream, or mass hysteria.

Such visions, moreover, are generated only when the recipients are in an agitated state of expectancy and in hopes of seeing their wishes fulfilled, a mood diametrically opposite from that of the disciples, who were hopelessly saturated in sorrow and despair. In fact, news of the resurrection nearly had to be forced on them in the face of their obvious disbelief.

And why, incidentally, did such visions ever end? The New Testament records of Jesus' appearances stop abruptly after forty days with the ascension, whereas such hallucinations might have continued for decades, centuries. Finally, this theory does not even touch the problem of an empty tomb.

The remaining hypotheses are so weak that they need no commentary. None of these theories, then, offers any solid base for historical reconstruction of what happened on the first Easter morning. If honestly examined, they appear quite fanciful, and all of them raise far more difficulties than they solve. No one theory explains all the phenomena reported at the time, and it would take an incredible combination of several of them to begin to do so. This much must be admitted, not merely on any basis of Christian apologetic, but of sober historical inquiry.

11

AN EMPTY TOMB

And they found the stone rolled away from the tomb, but when they went in they did not find the body.

LUKE 24:2–3

CAN HISTORY TELL US what *actually* happened on that crucial dawn?

Many facts from antiquity rest on just one ancient source, while two or three sources in agreement generally render the fact unimpeachable. In the case of the first Easter, there are at least *seven* ancient sources—the four gospels, Acts, and the letters of Paul and Peter—but this has not led to universal acceptance of the resurrection as a datum of history. Why not? Because the more unlikely the story, the stronger the evidence demanded for it. So if something supernatural were claimed, the evidence required to support it would have to be of an unimpeachable, absolute, and, indeed, direct eyewitness nature. Quite obviously, however, such categorical evidence disappeared with the death of the last eyewitnesses nineteen centuries ago.

Nevertheless, important historical evidence—quite apart from the Gospels—can be assembled to show that *the tomb, at any rate, was empty on Easter morning.* It should be added immediately that an empty tomb does not prove a resurrection, although a resurrection would require an empty tomb. Its occupancy, indeed, would effectively disprove it.

What happened in Jerusalem seven weeks after Easter could only have taken place if Jesus' body were missing from Joseph's sepulcher. For, beginning at the festival of Pentecost and continuing in the weeks thereafter, Peter and the other apostles sustained personality transformations inexplicable apart from their blazing faith in the resurrection. Abandoning their craven fear of the Jerusalem authorities, they began preaching a resurrected Christ with almost reckless boldness from no less a forum than the Temple itself. To Christians, what changed these men is itself a proof of the resurrection, and a chapter could be devoted to this phenomenon alone. But it is the reaction of the priestly authorities that, even for the neutral historian, must constitute evidence for an empty tomb. The Temple establishment did *not* do the obvious to counter the apostles' preaching: they did not lead an official procession out to Joseph's tomb, where, for all to see, they could have given the death blow to the dramatically growing kernel of Christianity by opening Joseph's sepulcher and revealing the moldering body of Jesus of Nazareth. They did not because they knew the tomb was empty, even if they had an official explanation for this: the disciples had stolen the body. But in offering this their admission was implicit: the sepulcher was vacant.

Some have tried to defeat this point by claiming that the disciples preached only a spiritual resurrection of the soul, with the body so unimportant that no one would have bothered to check a still-occupied tomb. This theory would be attractive for a Greek background, where philosophers taught the immortality of the soul, but not among Jews who believed that the resurrection was nothing if it did not involve the body.

This objection must now inevitably arise: But the record of the apostles' preaching a resurrected Jesus and the supposed failure of the authorities to produce the body rests only on New Testament sources biased in favor of Christianity. True, it rests on them, but not *only* on them. Some important, yet long overlooked, evidence derives also from purely Jewish sources and traditions.

Jewish Evidence

Understandably, this was hostile to Christianity, yet in none of the early Jewish writings is the statement made that the body of Jesus was still in its tomb that Sunday morning. Rather, Jewish polemic shared with Christians the conviction that the sepulcher was empty, but gave natural explanations for it. And such positive evidence from a hostile source is the strongest kind of evidence. For example, if Cicero, who despised Catiline, admitted that the fellow had one good quality among a host of bad ones—courage —then the historian correctly concludes that Catiline was at least courageous.

Some Jewish sources treat the matter neutrally. One of the earliest and most authoritative historians of this age was Josephus, whose celebrated reference to Jesus in *Antiquities* xviii, 3, 3, states, in part, "He was the Christ . . . for he appeared alive again on the third day." Since it is extremely unlikely that any Jew could have written this statement, it is properly regarded as an early Christian interpolation today. In 1972, however, Professor Schlomo Pines of Hebrew University in Jerusalem announced his finding of an Arabic manuscript with a differing and perhaps original version of this passage, which states, "His disciples . . . reported that he had appeared to them three days after his crucifixion and that he was alive; accordingly, he was perhaps the Messiah. . . ." This is language a Jew might have written with less difficulty, but what no one has yet pointed out is the remarkable fact that Josephus does *not* seek to scotch the resurrection claim by any information at his disposal that Jesus' body still lay in its grave. Certainly this is an argument from silence, but the silence is especially eloquent in view of Josephus' known habit of roasting false Messiahs elsewhere in his books.

Well into the second century A.D. and long after Matthew recorded its first instance, the Jerusalem authorities continued to admit an empty tomb by ascribing it to the disciples' stealing the

Tombs of the wealthy in this era were hewn out of rock and closed by a cylindrical stone, often a millstone, set in a channel. The tomb of Joseph of Arimathea in which Jesus was buried was undoubtedly very much like this sepulcher at Abu-Gosh west of Jerusalem, the ancient Kiriath-Jearim where the Ark of the Covenant remained for a time (I Sam. 7).

body. For, in his *Dialogue with Trypho,* Justin Martyr, who came from neighboring Samaria, reported c. 150 A.D. that the Jewish authorities even sent specially commissioned men across the Mediterranean to counter Christian claims with this explanation of the resurrection.

Early Jewish traditions regarding Jesus were later gathered also in a fifth-century compilation called the *Toledoth Jeshu,* which offers a garbled but interesting version of Jesus' burial. The disciples planned to steal the body of Jesus so they could claim a resurrection, the *Toledoth* states. But Juda, a gardener, overheard

Fishermen on the Sea of Galilee, looking north toward Magdala, home of Mary Magdalene.

their plans, and so he dug a grave in his own garden, stole Jesus' corpse from Joseph's tomb, and then laid it in the newly dug pit. When the disciples came to the original sepulcher and found it empty, they proclaimed Jesus' resurrection in Jerusalem. The Jews, who also found the tomb empty, were perplexed and in mourning until Juda wondered why everyone was so long-faced. Upon learning the cause, he smiled and conducted them to his garden where he unearthed the body of Jesus. Overjoyed, the priestly authorities asked Juda to give them the body, but he said, "No, I'll sell it to you." "How much?" they asked. "Thirty pieces of silver," came the reply. The priests gladly paid it, and then dragged the body of Jesus through the streets of Jerusalem.

It must be stated that Jewish scholars today regard the *Toledoth Jeshu* with total disdain, but the fact remains that this compilation, which reflects early traditions, the Talmud, and the fourth-century Jewish historian Josippon, agrees that Jesus' original tomb was empty.

Roman Evidence?

Provincial governors in the Roman Empire had to dispatch *acta* —annual reports of their activities—to the emperor, and Justin Martyr claims that Pilate mentioned the case of Jesus in his records prepared for Tiberius. But these have never been found, possibly due to the destruction of government archives in the great fire of Rome in 64 A.D.

Some scholars think that Pilate *may* have included a reference in his *acta* to the empty sepulcher along with a natural explanation for it—Jesus' body having been stolen—because a fascinating inscription was found in Nazareth on a 15-by-24-inch marble slab that might have been prompted by Tiberius' reply to Pilate. The inscription is an edict against grave robbery, and was written in Greek (italics mine):

> Ordinance of Caesar. It is my pleasure that graves and tombs remain perpetually undisturbed for those who have made them for the cult of their ancestors or children or members of their house. If, however, anyone charges that another has either demolished them, or has in any other way *extracted the buried, or has maliciously transferred them to other places in order to wrong them, or has displaced the sealing or other stones,* against such a one I order that a trial be instituted, as in respect of the gods, so in regard to the cult of mortals. For it shall be much more obligatory to honor the buried. Let it be absolutely forbidden for any one to disturb them. In case of violation I desire that the offender be sentenced to capital punishment on charge of violation of sepulture.

All previous Roman edicts concerning grave violation set only a large fine, and one wonders what presumed serious infraction could have led the Roman government to stiffen the penalty precisely in Palestine and to erect a notice regarding it specifically in Nazareth or vicinity. If only the "Caesar" had identified himself, but most scholars conclude—from the style of lettering in the inscription—that the edict derives from Tiberius or Claudius, either of whom *might* have reacted to tidings of the Easter enigma in Jerusalem. Nothing conclusive, however, has thus far been discovered from Roman sources.

Other Evidence

What happened to the Christian movement itself speaks strongly for an empty tomb. The seedbed for the first budding and growth of the church was in the city of Jerusalem itself, where, of all places, it would have been ridiculous to preach a risen Christ unless both the apostles and their hearers knew that Joseph's sepulcher was empty. Some months later, the authorities were so desperate to stop the movement that they even resorted to persecution. A far more effective tool would have been at least an elaborate counter-rumor that there was a body in Joseph's grave, but this was never attempted because by then there were apparently too many Jerusalemites who had seen for themselves that the sepulcher was empty at the time.

Accordingly, if all the evidence is weighed carefully and fairly, it is indeed justifiable, according to the canons of historical research, to conclude that the tomb of Joseph of Arimathea, in which Jesus was buried, was actually empty on the morning of the first Easter. And no shred of evidence has yet been discovered in literary sources, epigraphy, or archaeology that would disprove this statement.

This is as far as history can go. Pursuing any answer to the fascinating question " *Why* was the tomb empty?" leads very simply to two kinds of answers: the sepulcher was empty due to 1) some natural cause, or 2) some preternatural cause.

If it were a natural cause, this must still be discovered, because none of the theories advanced thus far is in any way probable or convincing. The empty tomb, in this interpretation, becomes one of the great, unresolved enigmas in history.

Christianity holds to the second alternative, that the tomb was

A shallow-draft fishing boat on the Sea of Galilee at sunrise.

empty due to Jesus' resurrection, which, of course, is what the New Testament proclamation is all about. But here also there is *some* supporting evidence outside the four Easter gospels. The psychological change of the disciples is certainly striking. What transformed Peter, the man who could be unhinged by questions from a servant girl into so bold a spokesman for the faith that even the entire Sanhedrin could not silence him? Had the disciples deceitfully tried to spawn a new faith on the world, would they have gone on to give their very lives for it? Clearly, they were themselves convinced that Jesus rose, for myths do not make martyrs.

The transformation of James the Just, Jesus' doubting brother, and of Paul, a convinced enemy of the fledgling church, is even more striking, and the conversion of the many Jerusalem priests mentioned in Acts 6:7 equally so.

One of the Jewish beliefs held with most tenacity is observance of the Sabbath, and yet Christian Jews transferred their worship from Saturday to Sunday, which they called "the Lord's Day." Only some drastic consideration would have introduced this change: their weekly celebration of the resurrection.

Finally, the birth and growth of the Christian church itself, its survival and expansion across nineteen centuries, offers telling evidence for the Easter event. Could it all have been rooted in a fraud, or did something else happen that Sunday dawn that has snared the belief of almost 800,000,000 people in the present generation alone?

The significance of the first Easter, in Christian theology, is its guarantee that Jesus did accomplish his mission of salvation and achieve the supreme "pilot project" for humanity in triumphing over the extreme enemy—death: Jesus rose; so will other human beings. No one expressed this better than someone who was not even around that morning. Paul wrote: "Since we believe that Jesus died and rose again, even so, through Jesus, God will bring to life with him those who have fallen asleep" (1 Thess. 4:14). This, the very earliest writing in the New Testament, dates from 50 A.D., only 17 years after the first Easter. Arguments that Christianity hatched its Easter myth over a lengthy period of time or that the sources were written many years after the event are simply not factual.

The defeat of death in renewed life, then, is the message of the first Easter, and of every celebration in the years since. Easter is the only festival that looks in two directions at the same time: back into history to fathom what happened in the week that changed the world, and forward into the future with the assurance that people who die will rise again. Small wonder that it was the earliest festival to be celebrated by the church, or that its message is as young as tomorrow.

NOTES

The familiar events of the Passion story and Easter are based on Matthew 21–28, Mark 11–16, Luke 19–24, John 11–21, and Acts 1. The lesser known episodes, references, and problems are documented below.

1. UP TO JERUSALEM

THE DISCIPLES: Lists of their names in Mt. 10:2–4; Mk. 3:16–19; Lk. 6:14–16; and Jn. 1:40 ff. suggest that Bartholomew may be identified with Nathanael, Thaddaeus with Judas (son of James), and Simon the Canaanean with Simon the Zealot.

THE DINNER AT BETHANY: Mt. 26:6 ff. and Mk. 14:3 ff. place the supper at the house of Simon the leper, while Jn. 12:1 ff. has it at the home of Mary, Martha, and Lazarus. Simon may have been husband to Mary or Martha, or their father.

2. INTRIGUE AND CONSPIRACY

PLOTS AGAINST JESUS: Instances before Holy Week include: Mt. 12:14; Mk. 3:6; Lk. 4:29, 6:11, 11:53, 13:31; Jn. 7:1, 7:25–45, 8:39 ff., 8:59, 10:31 ff., 11:46 ff., 12:10.

THE ARREST NOTICE: But for the caption and the last sentence, this proclamation is verbatim from the tradition on "Yeshu Hannosri" in *Sanhedrin* 43a of the Babylonian Talmud, trans. by Jacob Shachter (London: Soncino Press, 1935), Nezikin V, p. 281. The last sentence derives from what is probably the NT version of this proclamation in Jn. 11:57.

3. A LAST SUPPER

JUDAS ISCARIOT: Still another opinion claims that Iscariot is Aramaic for "liar" or "hypocrite," which was added to Judas' name afterwards. The fact that Simon Iscariot was his father, however, militates against this view.

THE CHRONOLOGY OF HOLY WEEK: The dates April 2, 33 A.D. for Maundy Thursday, April 3 for Good Friday, and April 5 for the first Easter are determined as follows. The most precisely given "anchor date" in the NT is Lk. 3:1–2, which states that John the Baptist began his public ministry "in the fifteenth year of the reign of Tiberius Caesar," i.e., 28–29 A.D. Adding a half to one full year for John's independent ministry and three and one-half for Jesus' would seem to require 32–33 A.D. as the year of the crucifixion. (The frequent explanation that Tiberius shared a co-regency with Augustus from 12 A.D. so that the fifteenth year of Tiberius could fall as early as 26 runs counter to all practice in the Roman sources, and is used only to salvage a thirty-year age for Jesus at the start of his ministry (Lk. 3:23), whereas, with birth in 5–4 B.C., he was at least 33 in fact. But Luke says "about 30", which would allow for such a range.) The specific date for Good Friday—April 3, 33 A.D.—is derived from the Jewish calendar. Ex. 12:6 states that the Passover lambs were slain on Nisan 14, and this date fell on a Friday only in April 7, 30 A.D., and April 3, 33 A.D., within the range of probability. The later date is preferable for reasons cited above and others. For further discussion, see Jack Finegan, *Handbook of Biblical Chronology* (Princeton, 1964), pp. 259 ff., and Paul L. Maier, "Sejanus, Pilate, and the Date of the Crucifixion," *Church History*, XXXVII (March, 1968), 1–11.

4. IN THE GARDEN

THE PASSOVER MOON: The Hebrew calendar was lunar, and the chief spring and fall festivals, the Passover and the Ingathering, commenced at full moon. Since Easter followed Friday, Nisan 14—the Passover date in the Jewish calendar that year—the Christian custom arose of celebrating Easter on the first Sunday after the first full moon occurring on or after the vernal equinox. Easter, thus, can fall anytime between March 22 and April 25.

5. ANNAS AND CAIAPHAS

ANNAS: Aside from the NT, references to Annas or Ananus appear also in Josephus, *Antiq.*, xviii, 2, 1; xx, 9, 1; and in *Pesachim* 57a of the Babylonian Talmud, the "Woe to the family of Annas" malediction.

CAIAPHAS: Aside from the NT, references to Caiaphas appear also in Josephus, *Antiq.*, xviii, 2, 1; and iv, 3.

TWO PROSECUTION WITNESSES NECESSARY: Deut. 19:15.

JUDICIAL PROCEDURE OF THE SANHEDRIN: See the Mishnah tractate *Sanhedrin*, iv, 1 to v, 5.

6. PONTIUS PILATE

THE PILATE INSCRIPTION: Antonio Frova, "L'Iscrizione di Ponzio Pilato a Cesarea," *Rendiconti Istituto Lombardo*, 95 (1961), 419–34. Although Pilate's proper title, prefect, has been known ever since 1961, the number of Biblical dictionaries and general encyclopedias published since then that perpetuate the mistaken term, procurator, is an embarrassment to serious scholarship.

THE AFFAIR OF THE STANDARDS: Josephus, *Antiq.*, xviii, 3, 1; *Wars*, ii, 9, 2–3. See also Carl H. Kraeling, "The Episode of the Roman Standards at Jerusalem," *Harvard Theological Review*, XXXV (October, 1942), 263–89.

THE AQUEDUCT RIOT: Josephus, *Wars*, ii, 9, 4; cp. also *Antiq.*, xviii, 3, 2.

THE GOLDEN SHIELDS: Philo, *De Legatione ad Gaium*, xxxviii, 299–305. See also Paul L. Maier, "The Episode of the Golden Roman Shields at Jerusalem," *Harvard Theological Review*, 62 (January, 1969), 109–21.

GESSIUS FLORUS: Josephus, *Wars*, ii, 14, 8.

PILATE'S FATE: The Samaritan episode is reported in Josephus, *Antiq.*, xviii, 4, 1–3. Origen, *Contra Celsum*, ii, 34, tacitly admits that Pilate suffered no penalty. See also Paul L. Maier, "The Fate of Pontius Pilate," *Hermes*, 99 (1971), 362–71. Portions of this and the next chapter appeared also in my article on Pilate in *Mankind*, II (February, 1970), 26 ff., and my book *Pontius Pilate* (New York: Doubleday, 1968).

7. A ROMAN TRIAL

THE CHARGE OF SORCERY: *Acta Pilati*, i; *Sanhedrin* 43a, the Babylonian Talmud.

"CAESAR'S FRIENDS": Suetonius, *Tiberius*, xlvi; Jn. 19:12. Cp. also Ernst Bammel, "Philos tou Kaisaros," *Theologische Literaturzeitung*, 77 (April, 1952), 206 ff.

RECENT CRITICISM OF NT ACCOUNTS OF THE TRIAL: S. G. F. Brandon, *Jesus and the Zealots* (New York: Scribner's, 1968); and *The Trial of Jesus of Nazareth* (New York: Stein and Day, 1968); Joel Carmichael, *The Death of Jesus* (New York: Macmillan, 1962); Haim Cohn, *The Trial and Death of Jesus* (New York: Harper & Row, 1971) and others. Some important thoughts in these studies go back to Robert Eisler, *The Messiah Jesus and John the Baptist* (New York: Dial, 1931).

RABBINICAL TRADITIONS ON JESUS AND ANNAS: *Sanhedrin* 43a and *Pesachim* 57a of the Babylonian Talmud. Various versions in the original and in translation of the *Toledoth Jeshu* are available in Samuel Krauss, *Das Leben Jesu Nach Jüdischen Quellen* (Berlin: S. Calvary & Co., 1902).

THE STONING OF JAMES: Josephus, *Antiq.*, xx, 9, 1. Ananus, the son of the NT Annas, was the high priest responsible for prosecuting James before the Sanhedrin in the absence of the Roman governor Albinus, who had not yet arrived in Judea.

8. AT SKULL PLACE

BONES OF THE CRUCIFIED VICTIM: N. Haas, "Anthropological Observations on the Skeletal Remains from Giv'at ha-Mivtar," *Israel Exploration Journal*, XX (1970), 38–59.

QUARRY SOUTH OF HOLY SEPULCHER: Kathleen M. Kenyon, *Jerusalem— Excavating 3000 years of History* (New York: McGraw-Hill, 1967), pp. 146 ff.

9. EASTER DAWN

"WHICH TWENTY MEN COULD SCARCELY ROLL": At Mt. 27:60, Codex Bezae adds: "And when he was laid there, he put against the tomb a stone which twenty men could scarcely roll." The Sahidic Ms. has this addendum also.

"THE SPICES": The hundred pounds cited in Jn. 19:39 were each about twelve of our ounces.

NOTES **127**

THE GRAVE CLOTHS: The first to call attention to the Greek in Jn. 20:6–7 indicating that Jesus "withdrew from the grave clothes without disturbing their arrangement" is Henry Latham, *The Risen Master* (London: G. Bell, 1904).

10. DOUBTS AND CRITICISM

"LETTUCE" THEORY: Tertullian, *De spectaculis*, xxx.

CELSUS AND SWOON THEORY: Origen, *Contra Celsum*, ii, 56. Celsus and the hallucination theory is Origen, *Ibid.*, ii, 55.

SLAVONIC JOSEPHUS: The reference to "thirty Romans but a thousand Jews" is vii, 4–8, in R. Dunkerley, *Beyond the Gospels* (Penguin, 1957).

THE IDENTITY OF THE GUARD at Joseph's sepulcher is by no means definite. Was it Jewish or Roman? The Greek of Mt. 27:65 cites Pilate's statement simply as: "You have a guard," though this could also be translated, "You may have a guard." Yet the first interpretation seems preferable, since the watch reported the empty tomb directly to the chief priests rather than Pilate (Mt. 28:11), which the Temple police would certainly have done. Roman auxiliaries would have reported to Pilate and only to him. Tertullian, *Apologeticus*, xxi, 20, also speaks of a Jewish military guard at the tomb.

SURVIVAL AFTER CRUCIFIXION: Josephus, *Vita*, 75.

STRAUSS CITATION: David F. Strauss, *The Life of Jesus for the People* (London: Williams & Norgate, 1879), I, 412.

MISCELLANEOUS OBJECTIONS TO THE EASTER ACCOUNTS: Aside from the problem of the variations, discussed in the text, there is the thorny issue of Jesus' own prediction that he would rise on the third day hardly being accommodated by his being in the grave only about thirty-six hours in purported fact. Yet there is no reason to tear up Holy Week and convert Good Friday into Good Wednesday, as some Biblical literalists have suggested. In Jewish practice, part of a day was counted as a whole day, and the three remaining hours of Friday afternoon following Jesus' death, plus Saturday, and the first twelve hours of Sunday (which began at 6 P.M. Saturday) would indeed add up to "the third day." Certainly, however, this would make only a very "rough fit" for Mt. 12:40 ("For as Jonah was three days and three nights in the belly of the whale, so will the Son of man be three days and three nights in the heart of the earth"). But this merely underlines the authenticity of the source material and lack of any editorial tampering. Surely Jesus' comment must not be subjected to ultra-literalism, for neither was he buried anywhere near the "heart of the earth."

11. AN EMPTY TOMB

APOSTOLIC PROCLAMATION IN JERUSALEM: Acts 2–8

JUSTIN: Justin Martyr, *Dialogue with Trypho*, 108.

JUDA THE GARDENER: This account from the *Toledoth Jeshu* appears in the Wagenseil text, the Strassburg Ms., and especially the Vindobona Ms. See Kraus, *op. cit.*, xiv-xv.

PILATE'S ACTA: Justin Martyr, *Apology*, I, xxxv, xlviii.

ROMAN EDICT ON GRAVE ROBBERY: F. Cumont, "Un Rescrit Imperial sur la Violation de Sèpulture," *Revue historique*, clxiii (1930), 241–66; and F. de Zulueta, "Violation of Sepulture in Palestine at the Beginning of the Christian Era," *Journal of Roman Studies*, xxii (1932), 184–97.